The Weekenders

By Max Gunther

The Weekenders

The Split-level Trap (with Dr. and Mrs. Richard Gordon)

The Weekenders

by MAX GUNTHER

With drawings by Susan Perl

J. B. Lippincott Company

PHILADELPHIA & NEW YORK

CONTENTS

The Weekenders

1. Who They Are

SOME PEOPLE hold celebrations to honor gods and spirits. We hold one every week to honor leisure. We call it the weekend. So hang up the bright ribbons and uncork the festive jug. Close the file cabinet, still the loud machine, bank the weekday fires. Let dour work now hide his ugly face. For this is the time when joy may come among us again.

The festival lasts two days, but the mood precedes it. The mood begins to be felt some time around noon on Friday. All over America at that hour life seems to gather momentum. On assembly lines and in offices, productivity, which has been climbing jerkily since Thursday, reaches its five-day peak. People hurry to finish assigned tasks before the workweek ends. Some are driven by a guilty feeling that they haven't yet paid heavily enough in sweat to buy two days off. Most are simply filled with a reborn enthusiasm about their work. It is like an irritating traveling companion who grows almost attractive as he prepares to get off the train and go away.

In luncheonettes, diners and plant cafeterias the noon crowds are restless and talkative. In the expensive restaurants patronized by the talent elite and its fringes, and on this day by office girls in self-conscious extravagance, rich food and drink crowd the undersized tables. More Scotch and bourbon, martinis and whiskey sours flow down the alimentary canal at this one meal than at any other, except, in some establishments, Saturday night dinner. Department stores are shunned by prudent housewives. Instead, the glittering aisles are thronged with working girls buying sportswear and datewear—leisure's costumes. They will be different people tomorrow. They must have different clothes.

In the suburbs and apartment neighborhoods homemakers crowd into beauty parlors where they can buy the look and sometimes the feel of youth, grace and gaiety, and perhaps a breath of sin too. For these also belong to the rites of the weekend. Supermarkets are crowded. So are liquor stores. Five-and-dime store managers patrol their aisles in happy frenzy as buyers clamor for party favors, bridge score cards, paper crockery and pretzels. The parking lot in which you could have landed an airliner yesterday has barely room for a Volkswagen today.

The faces are bright. The chatter is bright. The air is charged with expectancy.

Friday afternoon roars down its course toward evening. The 4:15 train and bus to the suburbs are more crowded than they were on the past four afternoons. The highways carry more homebound pool cars. Some of these early celebrants wear a proud and satisfied look, for the privilege of leaving work at four is a franchise of high rank. Others look furtive. Here is a man who has scuttled to a seat on the train and hides there behind his trembling newspaper. He has seen his superior in the crowd behind him, about to board the same car. He will not reap the full potential harvest of peace and joy from the weekend ahead. A few others are pinched with worry. Some are sunk in gloom.

But for most the augury seems bright.

Not for everybody, of course. Many face more work tomorrow. Some will return to their plants and office buildings. Some carry attaché cases full of work they must do, or believe they

must do, or secretly want to do (they will utter the ritual complaints, of course) at home over the weekend. Still others, notably housewives, have occupations whose demands do not cease, but can only be lightened somewhat, on Saturday and Sunday. And many must work for purposes of the festival. Saturday will find the supermarket manager and the five-and-dime man still prowling their aisles. The liquor merchant will still be there amid his euphoric fluids. The corner cop and his colleagues will work harder during the next thirty-six hours than in any other period of the week. They will break up fights, quiet noisy parties, attend to the victims of car accidents and haul in high-volume customers of the liquor merchant.

But the majority are looking forward to some sort of freedom from work over the next two days. Most of the employed are on their way home by six o'clock Friday evening. Some have stopped for drinks, but they can still be said to be on the way. Ahead now lies a vast fruited plain of free time. There are sixty-three hours to go until nine o'clock Monday morning —sixty-three hours in which the requirements of the struggle for survival are at least partially suspended. The week has reached its climax. The weekend is here.

For the majority, Friday evening is the transition period from work to leisure. A metamorphosis now begins to take place. It is complete by Saturday morning. The men and women who awake on Saturday morning are not the same people they were yesterday. The clothes they put on are different. Their moods, their feelings about themselves and others, their approach to life—all are different. For two days they will have about them a quality which is distinctly unlike anything they had on Friday or will have again on Monday.

They are almost infinitely various, of course, these Saturday-Sunday people. One of the great satisfactions of being human is that no two of us are alike. Yet when people live together in a society, mutually influencing and being influenced, they are bound to develop shared traits which in time can be recognized as characteristic of that society. So it is with the Saturday-Sunday people. Various as they are, they have some notable similarities. They share traits that don't show up as strongly or indeed at all during the rest of the week. So distinct are these traits, so different are these people from their workday selves, that we can give them a label all their own. We can call them the *weekenders*.

Weekenders are to be found in every state. They are predominantly metropolitans. They live in cities, suburbs and the semirural fringes immediately beyond. They are part of the great bunching of population in advancing industrial nations. Some 57 per cent of Americans lived in metropolitan areas in 1940, but now the figure is 70 per cent and still climbing. People in metropolia are linked with each other in vast complexity. They can no longer work and play according to the rhythms of personal mood or need but are all bound to the same gigantic rhythm: five days on, two off.

Of course metropolitan areas differ, and so do districts within each area. This creates differences and degrees of difference in the weekenders' outward behavior. A suburbanite with a quarter-acre plot to maintain doesn't do the same things on Saturday as a city dweller, who may believe creeping red fescue is some kind of loathsome tropical disease. The city dweller casually visits restaurants and theaters which are a big deal to the suburbanite. Weekend activities follow one pattern in a giant metropolis like New York, another in a city like Seattle with its nearly unlimited horizons of natural playground, still another in a small compact city like Tulsa with open farm country but a short drive from downtown. Some cities and suburbs have more recreational and cultural real estate than others. Some have more nightclubs. Some have more active churches. Some have more available sin. All these elements shape the weekenders' choices of things to do. Yet from Seattle to New York, from Nightlife Square to the quasi-rural fringes of outer suburbia, the basic framework of choice is similar.

The weekender is typically a middle-class man or woman. He is among the vast majority of Americans who range from lower white-collar through upper no-tie to upper button-down, and aim higher. Many of his outstanding traits also show up among unskilled laborers' families and in the upper strata of society, among those with inherited wealth. But the weekender reaches his fullest and finest expression in the middle classes, among people who are comfortable but must work to stay so. He has a car, a TV set, three kinds of breakfast cereal, a share of General Motors, an electric can opener and a large feeling of insecurity. The middle classes are what America is all about, after all. Their huge number is a result of the same industrial growth that created the weekend. They dominate the American scene. National advertising is aimed at them almost exclusively, except in a few specialized media. Magazines, newspapers, books and TV shows are created largely by middle-class people for middle-class people. Far more than those at the two ends of the income scale they influence and are influenced on a countrywide scale.

Weekenders also differ in age and marital status. But this again creates only outward differences in their behavior. High school and college youngsters are weekenders in training. Particularly in college they conduct their sometimes bizarre weekend affairs for basically the same reasons that impel their parents. They do it with less finesse, of course. This gives their elders the opportunity to make sarcastic remarks about them. But what adults jeer at is usually just an exuberant extension of their own fits and fancies.

So much for the gross differences among weekenders. The similarities, the shared traits that distinguish weekenders from workday people, are not as immediately obvious. We'll have to probe the weekender's head and heart to see them. But there are outward stigmata. Perhaps the most evident is the furiousness of the weekender's activity.

Weekends are generally thought of as days set aside for leisure. Leisure, though it has many definitions, generally implies a rather peaceful kind of activity or no activity at all. But either weekends will have to be reexamined or the word leisure will have to be redefined once more. Peace is nowhere in the weekend picture—or, if it is there, lies somewhere in a corner obscured by dust and turmoil. The weekenders golf, ski, bowl and boat. They dance, tell jokes and make love. They drink standing up and sitting down. They go to theaters, art galleries and concerts. They play with their children, go to church and sell dented brass candlestick holders at PTA bazaars. They build things, repair things, paint things and plant things. Many a business official has said he'd be pleased if the weekday people threw themselves into their work with half that much spirit. Lemuel Boulware put it succinctly when he was vice-president and personnel chief of General Electric. "It is not this company's policy," said he plaintively, "to send people home on Friday as tired as they come in on Monday."

The nature of this Monday fatigue has not been fully explored. Is it the satisfying ache of bone and muscle after hard use? The contented slump of the mind after some goal has been achieved? Or is it the irritable kind of fatigue that comes from a buildup of small unrelieved tensions and frustrations? These questions are worth asking. The weekend is a tremendous opportunity for the pursuit of happiness. It stretches over more than one-fourth of the week, a great double handful of free time in which each of us theoretically can seek whatever will make him content.

Not only is the expenditure of energy enormous on weekends, but so is the expenditure of money. The United States government estimates its people spend about $40 billion a year on recreation, and probably at least two-thirds of this staggering total is contributed by the sleepless weekenders. That is a lot of dollars. If laid end to end these dollars would stretch from here to—well, quite a long way. Americans, largely weekenders, also drink about a quarter of a billion gallons of distilled spirits a year. That is enough to lay the entire population of Greater Los Angeles end to end.

Another of the weekenders' visible stigmata is their intense wanderlust. They travel restlessly within their metropolia all weekend. They go to museums, zoos, restaurants, country clubs and antique auctions. They visit each other. They also travel out of metropolia Friday night and back in Sunday afternoon. Sometimes they travel out and in on a single day. Their restlessness creates enormous problems on the highways. They have more accidents than anybody. The National Safety Council says an average Tuesday or Wednesday in 1960 saw 81 deaths in automobile accidents across the nation. But an average Friday saw 110, an average Saturday 154 and an average Sunday 125.

According to the Safety Council these macabre weekend statistics can't be blamed solely on increased traffic. Weekend fatigue plays a large part. Most accidents occur in the evening hours when people are driving home after a day at the beach or the ski slopes or the camping grounds, often with tired, quarrelsome children in the car. And there is another element to be considered, a more elusive one. Something goes wrong with people's car-handling judgment on weekends. Highway police notice it and vastly prefer a midweek tour of duty. Weekend traffic has a brittle aggressive quality. Drivers seem to be going at high speed even when their cars are stopped dead in a typical weekend jam. They are irritable, easily angered, easily tempted into high-horsepower foolishness. Small mistakes and discourtesies by other drivers make them seethe with rage.

What are the causes behind these symptoms? Why does the weekender drive himself to exhaustion? Why the tremendous outpouring of money? Why all the wandering about, jittery and fretful? Some inner devil seems to be goading the weekender. He seems to be searching for something. It must be a thing of desperate importance, more important to him perhaps than his work. If an employer asked him to put in hours like these, he would resign indignantly.

The weekender is in search of an emotional aura. It is a sweet, sweet feeling that has come over him occasionally on weekends past, a sense of peace and blessedness that told him he hadn't worked all week in vain. He isn't quite sure what this feeling is and usually can't define it, but he knows he will recognize it when he finds it. It has no convenient label. Call it the feeling of living the good life.

On Friday night the weekender vaguely senses the nearness of this aura. He knows it waits for him, large and lovely, somewhere in the expanse of time between here and Monday. It is his, if only he has the wit to grasp it. O to recapture the feeling of the good life, just for a day, just for an hour!

If pressed for a definition, the weekender might apply any of a number of labels. His idea of the good life, he might say, would be a life of leisure. The word leisure as used in advertising means simply time away from work and refers to anything that can be used or consumed in that time, like barbecue sets and shuttlecocks. Other users of the word insist that it refers to a state of mind, not of employment. At any rate it suggests tranquility, an easygoing kind of happiness and an absence of everyday pressures. These qualities certainly are included in the weekender's thoughts about the good life. They are part of the aura for which he yearns on Friday night.

Rutgers University Professor Sebastian de Grazia in 1962 finished a monumental study, *Of Time, Work and Leisure,* for the Twentieth Century Fund. In it he suggests the Greeks in the age of Pericles perfected the art of leisure, raising it to a height that has not been reached since. The Greeks' idea of leisure was woven into the idea of intellectual endeavor, but it seems also to have had subtle emotional overtones. Dr. de Grazia describes the emotional quality of the Greek life as "a state of being fed with love and song." This, too, is part of the weekender's yearning.

Searching for other ways to describe the good life, he might include the idea of gracious living. This, like leisure, is an-

other phrase that has gone out of focus, if it was ever in. It
is an advertising gimmick that came to prominence some time
in the late 1940's. It has been used to sell furniture, wine, grass
seed, hotel accommodations, meals in restaurants and almost
everything except sewer pipe. But it is useful for labeling a
mode of weekend thought. It suggests ease and great wealth.
The kind of wealth it suggests is the laudable kind, gentle and
cultured rather than gross. According to Hollywood and its
supporting novelists, gracious living was enjoyed by the owners
of Southern plantations before the Civil War. Pillared porches,
rolling lawns, mint juleps, conversations about literature, ball
gowns and horseback riding are considered gracious. Gracious
living has a faint Latin flavor. All rich Italians, Spaniards and
Frenchmen live graciously, but rich Germans, Englishmen and
Americans don't. New Orleans and San Francisco are sometimes
referred to as gracious cities, but New York and Chicago never
are. Wine and espresso coffee are gracious.

The feeling of gracious living is one of knowing what the
good things of life are and knowing how to enjoy them. It is
the feeling of being surrounded by costly things but being so
thoroughly at home among them that you cannot be charged
with ostentation. The gracious-living man serves sirloin steak
and pours wine in such a way that his guests think these are
his ordinary fare. He is not scared of French waiters. He re-
veals without seeming to think it noteworthy that he is a
patron of theater, concert hall and art gallery. He surveys his
living room and its furnishings with manifest pleasure while
seeming at the same time to take them for granted. In short he
is the personification of self-indulgence, but he somehow makes
it utterly praiseworthy.

Gracious living is a weekend frame of mind. It overlaps and
perhaps includes the concept of leisure. The weekender pursues
it ardently, for it is part of his vision of the good life.

Another element he would probably mention is that of full-
ness. The good life as he envisions it would be a well-rounded

one like that of the ideal many-faceted man in the Italian Renaissance. This is perhaps his reaction to the increasing specialization required in the modern workday world. He doesn't believe narrowness is a good thing. He wants to taste everything life offers. Everything pleasant, that is. He envisions a life of tranquility shot through with intense joyful experiences. He wants to be quietly cultured but also capable of high jinks.

An art patron and a water skier, an idler by sylvan streams and a whooper-up at parties, a churchgoer and a sinner.

Well-roundedness has been a national ideal for a long time. Colleges spoon out liberal arts to their engineering students, and liberal arts students are urged to get a dash of science. Business conventions usually have at least one speaker who tells the assembled executives they ought to read Shakespeare. Some years ago *Mademoiselle* Magazine asked its sophisticated young readers, mainly college and career girls and young housewives, how they defined success. They defined it mainly as well-roundedness. They scorned the old-fashioned dream of fame and fortune. What they wanted was a full, happy life, be it ever so humble (though not too humble). They wanted happy husbands and happy children, homes gracious but not ostentatious, tennis and swimming, Mozart, gay parties, PTA meetings, sculpture lessons and serious discussions of birth, death and infinity.

Russell Lynes, who wrote a report on the survey, was struck by this "devotion to well-roundedness." The American dream, he wrote, is "of developing as many of one's potentialities as possible without letting any of them run away with the others." The young women shied away from the thought of becoming so absorbed in careers that they would fail as wives and mothers. Conversely they didn't want to be just Moms either. They were horrified at the spectacle of a husband so concerned with getting ahead that he neglected the other things life offers. Life to them was a vast smorgasbord. They wanted to nibble at everything on the table. They proposed to do most of this nibbling on weekends. The weekend is the time when the modern specialized metropolitan can do his well-rounding.

This multicolored vision of the good life is the hazy distant goal that keeps the weekender searching, ever searching. It is an elusive goal because it isn't a thing but a complex, subtle feeling. He must work hard to find it.

But the elusiveness of the goal is not the only reason why the weekender goes without sleep. He has only two days in which to pursue his quest.

He may sometimes find something akin to his vision of the good life on a workday, but he doesn't expect it. He looks to the weekend for the justification of his life. The weekend is the focus and climax of his week's existence. It is what he is alive for.

Life to the weekender is like skiing. From Monday to Friday he climbs uphill. The climb is a necessary part of the sport and may even be pleasant, but it isn't the essence. The essence is in the (he hopes) swift exhilarating run which the climb makes possible. The weekend is what everything is all about.

Indeed it may be that the weekenders are what Americans are all about. "Tell me what a man does in his leisure and I will tell you what sort of man he is," Samuel Johnson once remarked. The weekenders are Americans in their moment of hope. Whatever Americans dream of doing or being, you'll find them trying to do it or be it on weekends. A housewife on workdays wears a faded housecoat and a faded face. She isn't likely to agree this is her real self. But on Saturday night you will find her pretty, witty and gay. On Saturday afternoon she may have gone to a club meeting and briefly become an executive. A career girl on workdays may feel she is indisinguishable from the thousands of other career girls who jostle her on bus, subway and sidewalk. On weekends she seeks to express her fuller personality by redecorating her apartment, perhaps, or being a siren at a dim-lighted dinner party, or even taking a married friend's children to the zoo. An executive on workdays may be troubled by a growing tightness in his clothes around the waist, a sense of poor muscle tone and other signs that his body isn't what it might be. He wonders how much man he is. He has a recurrent daydream in which he chucks it all in favor of some hard physical life—buys a marina, maybe, or joins the Peace Corps. On weekends he eases his self-doubts by becoming a manual laborer or an athlete.

Each expresses his own longings in his own way. Each would give highly individual details if asked to describe his version of the perfect weekend. Yet all are searching for the same emotional stage setting, the aura of joy-splashed peace and gentle self-indulgence. Every Friday evening there begins a mass quest for the good life.

So fill the festive gas tank, polish the goblets and crank up the pastoral lawnmower. The good life awaits. Seize it, seize it if you can.

2. The Several Faces of Time

SINCE THE BEGINNING of the industrial age and perhaps since the dawn of history, men have dreamed of a heaven such as this. Imagine having two whole days every week when you don't have to struggle for survival! Two regularly scheduled, absolutely guaranteed days! The United States was the first industrial nation to give the majority of its people this gift. Sometimes other nations have been jealous of it. Sometimes we've felt vaguely guilty and wondered whether we deserved it, but most often we've been proud to own it. Industrial leaders have been particularly enthusiastic in praising the two-day weekend. They point to it whenever they want to convince workers there is nothing to fear in automatic machinery. "Look what machines have done for you," they urge. "Look at all the free time you've gained!"

It sounds delightful. The weekend at first glance does indeed look like a solid chunk of free time, a beautifully pure chunk, stoutly walled off from the work that leans against either end. But the weekender may question the word "free" in this highly praised free time. It puzzles him. Looking back over his last weekend, he senses that it was almost as full of obligations as the workweek. Instead of stepping off the treadmill on Friday night and drifting in freedom for two days, he simply changed treadmills.

We are a masochistic society. We enjoy vivisecting ourselves
and sneering at our own innards. Perhaps this is fun. It's undoubtedly useful when we find something than can be repaired
or improved. If the weekender feels his free time to be less free
than it looks, perhaps some of the causes are in his own head
and heart. But we shouldn't ignore other possible causes. Some
of these are distinctly not the weekender's fault. Some are built
into the very structure of the weekend itself.

Perhaps the most baffling of them is the fact that weekend
time is clocked time. Clocked time was invented at the beginning of the industrial age to serve work. Free time had no
choice but to tag along and be clocked too.

We often fail to see the curse of clockedness. We're used to
it. It's hard for us to imagine that, as late as the eighteenth
century and for all time before that, the great mass of people
lived without clocks and without caring whether it was two
o'clock or three o'clock, let alone whether it was 2:15 or 2:30.

There was no need for clocks. People worked as individuals
or in small groups. A man got up in the morning and thought:
Well, today I'll finish joining the legs of that bench. He ate his
breakfast and went to work. After a few hours, maybe, it occurred to him that he hadn't seen his friend Roger the mason for
a long time. So he put down his tools and ambled over to
Roger's place. Roger, leading a similarly loose-scheduled life,
was happy to see his friend, the joiner. They went over to the
tavern for a companionable cup. Pretty soon they felt hungry,
so they went back home to eat. Maybe the joiner felt sleepy
after that. He napped for a while. Then he went back to work.

Possibly he worked till sundown. Possibly he put in an eight-
hour day, or twelve or sixteen hours. He didn't know. Perhaps
he didn't care. Time for him was only a progression from dawn
to dusk, from youth to age.

Whether the unclocked craftsman or sailor or farmer had
more or less free time than we have today is a question over
which scholars are still arguing. Nobody really knows. Dr. de

Grazia of the Twentieth Century Fund believes at least some of the old-time unclocked people had as much time off the job as we so proudly boast today. Sunday or the Sabbath as a non-work day has of course been characteristic of Christian and Hebrew countries for centuries. The second day off is a recent innovation, but in parts of medieval Europe—and during cer-

tain periods in ancient Rome—there were more than a hundred religious holidays and festivals a year. Whether the majority of people customarily abandoned their tools for the entire day during such a festival is, again, an unanswered question. Probably it varied with the individual and the work group. Some may have worked most of the day and attended the singing and dancing at night. Others may have got howling drunk and needed the following day to recover.

But the point isn't whether we have more or less free time than people in preindustrial days. The point is that our beloved two-day weekend is a different kind of free time. The unclocked man and woman lived a life in which work and free time were mixed in random fashion, like peas and carrots. He worked when he had to or felt he should, took time off when his hunger or greed or master let him. By contrast our weekend is an ordained and immovable period of free time. It starts and ends at precise hours not set by our own moods or wishes.

It has to be like this, of course. An industrial society couldn't easily operate otherwise. When the first crude production lines began to appear in England in the eighteenth century, it became obvious that men working as a team in conjunction with machines could no longer take their free time when the mood seized them. Men and machines had to start together and stop together. This rule grew more rigid as the machines and factories and work forces grew bigger and more complicated. Costly, fuel-hungry machines couldn't be started by the first few men who arrived for work and then allowed to spin flywheels idly until the rest of the crew wandered in from breakfast. Foundry furnaces couldn't economically be banked or shut down in the middle of the day while the crew went away to dance about a Maypole. It became necessary for men to stay at work once they got to the factory. They had to work steadily through the day with only brief rests. If, somewhere along the production line, a man ambled away from his station to have a beer or even stopped work for a minute to watch a butterfly outside the window, the whole system might collapse.

The clock that rules our lives had begun to tick. In England, then elsewhere in Europe, then in the United States, the old unclocked ways of life began to break down under the impact of the industrial machine. Farm workers by the thousands lined up at factory gates to ask for jobs. So did craftsmen who could no longer compete with the machine products' prices. So did women and children. In the three decades between 1860 and 1890 the number of nonfarm employees in the United States—potential weekenders—actually tripled.

When all these people applied at plant and office for their jobs, they were told something that should have bothered them more than it apparently did. They were told they'd have to work anywhere from sixty to eighty hours and usually six but sometimes seven days a week. Factory owners felt they had little choice about this. The early machines had to be worked hard if they were to pay for themselves. And business conditions in the infant industrial society were chaotic. No businessman could predict how long his products would sell profitably. The dominant management philosophy of the day was to work men and machines furiously while the demand held up, then close the plant when the market collapsed.

The job applicants don't seem to have been notably startled by the sixty- to eighty-hour demand. After all, most of them were used to working from dawn to dusk. Probably few had ever

stopped in their previous lives to count the hours of actual work they did in an average day or week, even those who owned clocks. But when the hiring boss said seventy hours, he meant seventy hours of solid work—not seventy hours during which you worked a little, sat and mused awhile, worked some more, chatted with a neighbor, worked some more.

The ticking of the clock grew louder with each passing year. The signal for the start of a day's work was no longer the grand, imprecise march of dawn up the eastern sky. From now on it was the exact and unlovely factory whistle or (in later years) the prim humorless jangle of the alarm clock.

Free time, what there was of it, now had to be doled out in measured chunks. At first these chunks were neither large nor frequent, as today's industrialists are fond of pointing out. Men, women and children sweated over howling machines for as long as fourteen hours a day. But then industry and its machines, which had robbed many people of free time, slowly began to give it back. As machines grew more efficient, workers could turn out more products in less time. Benevolent industrialists and wary unions saw to it that this gain was returned at least in part to the workers—some of it in money, some in free time. The average manufacturing workweek in the United States shrank from about 60 hours in 1900 to 39.7 hours in 1960.

Thus we got our free time back—at least a good portion of it and possibly more than anybody had ever had before. We got a two-day weekend. But it is still clocked time.

Clocked. Perhaps on Friday we are absorbed in a project that grips our attention. We want to go on working. But we must abandon the project for two days, for now the weekend is here. It is Saturday. We have nothing we particularly wish to do with this free time on this particular day, but the clock and calendar say we can't go to work. So we mope about, feel futile, grumble at everybody in sight and go to bed with the feeling of a day wasted. Sunday comes and goes uselessly, and then it is Monday. On Monday after lunch, perhaps, something other than work catches our thoughts. A spring breeze is blowing, reminding us of a hillside where we might lie and watch the clouds. Or a boy passes carrying ice skates. We want to follow. But we can't. Today is a workday.

The aura of good living that weekenders seek can't easily be summoned up at will. The best times we ever have are the spontaneous ones when the precious feeling comes unbidden and unexpected. It doesn't automatically ride the buses and trains home on Friday evening. It doesn't live comfortably in a clocked society. As Dr. de Grazia says of the leisurely state of mind, it requires "a sense of unlimited time"—time such as the unclocked man and woman must often have enjoyed.

The nature of his free time forces the weekender into an effort that is bound to fail more times than not. He can't wait for the leisurely state of mind to come around by itself, for it's as likely to come on Wednesday as Saturday. So he tries to bulldoze it into existence by a massive assault of money and energy. This can't always be counted on to work. When you try to cram joys between deadlines, you usually reap nothing but exhaustion.

And the damnable clock ticks on right through our freest periods of free time. We're so used to obeying it that we're its slaves even when we don't have to be. I remember strolling on an Atlantic beach one blustery September weekend. My little boy was with me. We were scaling clamshells into the onshore wind and watching them curve back to us. I don't know why this was fun. It isn't the kind of activity you could make money from. If an entrepreneur set up a Clamshell Scalerama (Test your skill! Healthful exercise! Fun for the whole family!), he'd be lucky to amortize the cost of his clamshells. But on that morning scaling clamshells seemed like the best of all possible things to do.

After a while I looked at my watch. It was lunch time. We left the beach reluctantly and walked up the road to eat. Only after I'd sat down at the table did I wonder what I was doing. What is so important about noon? Why must we follow the same eating schedule on weekends that we follow, not having a choice, on workdays? The clock has us hypnotized.

My boy and I went back to the beach after lunch. But the mood was gone. The clamshells and the wind did nothing for us now but blow sand in our eyes.

The curse of clockedness is only one problem of weekend time. Here is another. Though the weekend seems solidly walled off from work, it isn't really that well built. Work is always leaking in from both ends.

They tell the story in Westwood, New Jersey, of a fellow who

went supermarketing one Saturday morning. It took him more than an hour to cull from the shelves all the items on his shopping list. He spent another half hour waiting in the checkout line. This wan't his favorite way of spending weekend time. When he finally got out of the supermarket he was quivering with barely controlled rage. He started to wheel his loaded basket along the sidewalk, found his way blocked by a flotilla of empty baskets, tried to smash his way through and ended cursing on the pavement beneath his groceries.

A Dr. Robert Gorman treated him for a severely sprained ankle and advised him to rest for a few days with his leg up. On Sunday night some friends dropped in for a drink. Somebody said it was too bad such an accident had to happen on a weekend. "Hell," the shopper said, "don't feel sorry for me. This was the best weekend I've ever had."

Things have come to a pretty pass when a man has to sprain an ankle in order to enjoy a restful weekend. Anyway, why was this unfortunate man shopping on Saturday? Why were all those other people in the supermarket to delay him? Blame it on work.

The nature of work in our industrial age requires people to gather each weekday in some central place. They must live near this workplace, but most don't like to live too near. Thus, especially in the suburbs, the housewife is left with some interesting difficulties. Her husband is away all day. Unlike housewives in preindustrial communities she has no mother or grandmother or other handy babysitter nearby. If she wants to go marketing, she takes the kids. The fact that courageous women sometimes do this doesn't alter the fact that it can't be done. So the wife waits until Saturday when her husband is home. Indeed he may have taken the car to work all week. All over America, and particularly in the suburbs, Saturday is shopping day.

There are some gloomy statistics in the files of the Mutual Broadcasting System on this perversion of free time. Some years ago MBS asked a market-research outfit, J. A. Ward, Inc., to find out in detail how people use their time. The result was *A Nationwide Survey of Living Habits*. It was never published, possibly because the good-hearted MBS and J. A. Ward felt it would make people unhappy.

See if this makes you unhappy. Women spend twice as much time shopping on an average Saturday as on any other day. Men spend three times as much.

So this free and lovely day, this day designed for living, becomes instead a focal point of the week's marketing. It is the day for major harvesting at the supermarket, for trips to department stores and appliance stores and furniture stores. Thus has work pushed into our clocked-off period of free time. An adult has certain requirements to fulfill every day, weekend or not. If the individual and his species are to survive, he must daily, or almost daily, eat, sleep and care for his young, if any. The duties may often be pleasant but they preclude the weekend's being a sixty-three-hour stretch of totally free time.

A clever wife may be able to arrange her week's work so that most of it is finished by Friday, but on the weekend there are still meals to prepare, beds to make and noses to wipe. If she is lucky or belligerent, her husband will help her with this kind of chore over the weekend, provided he can spare time from his "fix-it" schedule. Thus she may get more freedom than she has during the week. But unless the family has servants, the weekend can't be the beautiful, untouched spread of time industrialists talk about when they're praising machines.

Childless families and the single escape the obligation of caring for the young. But work has other ways of stealing weekend freedom. Consider Friday evening. The employed man or woman finishes work at, say, five thirty. But he isn't free yet. He must now spend time getting away from the central workplace where his presence is required on weekdays. The city dweller may reach home in fifteen minutes or half an hour if the rapid-transit system is rapid that night. The suburbanite may not make it until seven o'clock or later. (If his job requires

distant travel, he may not arrive until past midnight.) Supper
takes till eight. The kids are in bed and the dishes washed by
nine. Now Friday evening is about half gone. Possibly husband
and wife are suffering from work hangover: fatigue, headache
and grumpiness. There is nothing for them to do but crumple
up morosely before the television set for a couple of hours and
then go to bed.

Now consider Sunday evening. What can we do in these last

fading hours of free time? At first glance they seem as free as the hours of Saturday night. But look ahead a few hours: eleven o'clock, midnight. See the ugly form of work lurking there in the shadows, skulking backward toward us from Monday morning. On Monday we must be up early. So we must go to bed early on Sunday night. No late parties, no late movies. Even weekend crime tapers off at 10 P.M. on Sunday. Sunday night isn't ours. A half interest in it belongs to work.

Do you want to know how much free time you really have in the sixty-three hours from Friday evening to Monday morning? Turn again to the rather tragic figures in Mutual Broadcasting's *Nationwide Survey*. These figures can't and don't show how much real contentment a typical man or woman might find. This is something that lives in the heart and probably can't be reliably discovered by a survey or translated into numbers. What a survey can show, however, is how many leisurelike activities people customarily engage in over a weekend. In the *Nationwide Survey* these included hobbies, spectatorship, reading, visiting or being visited, playing games and going to church.

The average man has 5.5 hours of this on Saturday and 7.9 on Sunday. The average woman has 5.3 hours on Saturday and 7.1 on Sunday. There are fewer leisure hours on a weekend day than there are work hours on a workday.

3. The Perspirational Approach

A WOMAN TELEPHONED a psychiatrist at three o'clock one Saturday morning and told him she was scared. When he asked what she was scared of, she said she didn't know. The doctor might have been forgiven if he'd hung up and grumpily gone back to sleep. But he didn't. He was Dr. Alexander Reid Martin, then chairman of the American Psychiatric Association's Standing Committee on Leisure Time and Its Uses. He'd spent much of his professional life studying people's reactions to what he calls "unstructured time." This was not the first patient he'd heard complain of diffuse fears at the beginning of a weekend.

The fears erupt in various ways. Another of Dr. Martin's patients was a business executive with a gastric ulcer. Every Friday evening as the work week neared its end, he suffered acute pain. The pain diminished somewhat when he went home but recurred in spasms throughout the weekend. Once he tried to take a vacation. The thought of several weeks' unstructured time produced gastric agony so intolerable that he went to a hospital instead.

Nearly all people in our society need work to hang their lives upon. Some need it more than others. Some need it so badly that when work is snatched away their lives start to disintegrate. With utter bewilderment each Friday night they face the enormous question of man's obligations and oppor-

tunities in the time left over from work. When a man's belly
is full and his family taken care of, what should he do? This
question concerned Plato, fascinated William James, perplexed Carlyle and has baffled millions of less articulate people
through all of history. What is a man or woman without work?
Some find themselves to be next to nothing. The weekend to
them is a desert to be crossed.

The ordinary weekender is somewhat happier about it. When
he reaches Monday, he may look back with some disappointment on the two days just past, but he doesn't usually think
of them as an ordeal. Still, if you ask him, "What do you do?"
he will tell you how he spends the workweek, not the weekend.
Work in our society is considered more important than play
and a more meaningful clue to a man's or woman's nature.
Knowing a man is an insurance salesman, you feel (mistakenly
perhaps) that you have him more strongly outlined than you
would knowing he is a bridge player or a visitor of zoos.

This is the weekender's dilemma. His weekend is important
to him, but he can't escape the nagging thought that maybe
it shouldn't be. He is likely to feel ill at ease when he is loafing.

No doubt this is one reason why he often fills his weekends with nonstop activity, for if you aren't working, the next most admirable thing is to be playing hard. And sometimes he simply comes to terms with himself by using his weekends for work.

The perspirational approach to weekends is a way of escaping the sometimes frightening emptiness of free time. Some weekenders adopt the approach more often than others, but most spend at least some of their Saturdays and Sundays at work. In the suburbs you see them toiling with hoe, spade, broom and paint brush. Some of the jobs they do are necessary and can only be done on weekends. Some aren't necessary at all.

Here is a housewife crawling about her lawn on her pretty knees, wrenching out crabgrass. Why? It is the custom in the suburbs not to like crabgrass, and possibly she feels so strongly about it that she can't rest until her esthetic sensibilities are satisfied. But actually crabgrass looks fine most of the time if mowed short, so it is more likely she is working just to be working. She is filling an emptiness of time. She is seeking a focus of some kind to dispel the feeling of being adrift. And here is a man painting the inside walls of his garage. What on earth is he doing that for? If there is anything that doesn't need painting, it is a garage. The man is doing it because he wants to work.

Suburban homeowners don't need to look hard to find weekend work. City dwellers and those in rented houses must often look outside the home. They wash cars a lot. In New York on Saturday afternoons some residential streets are so crowded with car washers that you can hardly go down the sidewalk without tripping over a bucket. "It's necessary," one biweekly washer explained. "All this soot in the air corrodes the paint and chrome if you don't get it off." This is just an excuse. Modern car paints are remarkably tough. Unless a car owner wants his beloved chariot to shine like diamonds, all he really need do is leave it out in a good rainstorm occasionally. "A car in most conditions only needs washing once or twice a year," a Chrysler engineer says. "Matter of fact, frequent washing can do more harm to the paint than good."

Crabgrass pulling and car washing of course may stem not only from a wish to work but from a desire to gain status by having the greenest lawn or the shiniest car. Other kinds of weekend work have little to do with status—cupboard emptying, for instance. This is a common Saturday occupation among women everywhere. One single girl living in a San Francisco apartment takes out all her dishes, silverware and knickknacks twice or three times a year, washes them, polishes them, disinfects the cupboards and drawers, puts everything back and collapses in self-righteous fatigue. This is her way of curing *Weltschmerz* and all other kinds of *schmerz*. "I do it when I'm

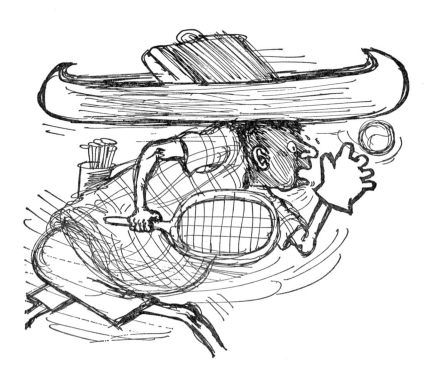

blue," she explained to a group of friends. "It helps me think."
Work is one of our society's oldest prescriptions for a troubled
mind.

A city-dwelling executive some years ago bought an acre of
woodland on the metropolitan fringe and set about building
himself a weekend house. Every weekend he and his wife drove
out there, put up at a nearby motel and worked on their acre.
It was to be a modernistic house of rather odd shape, designed
by a young architect (the executive's nephew) who mistook
asymmetry for art. Two of the walls were of masonry rather
than frame construction. Masonry is among the hardest of all
skilled trades, and no amateur should attempt a large job until
he has practiced on at least a few small ones. But the executive
attempted it anyway. He spent his weekends covered with
sweat and concrete dust. He went to his office Monday mornings with blistered hands and a beatific look. He had to stop
when winter closed in. Next spring as he prepared to start again
he found the local building inspector contemplating the property with a mournful air.

"Sorry," said the inspector, "but you'll have to have these
walls knocked down." Not only had winter frost cracked open
some of the imperfect bonds but the walls were several degrees
out of plumb.

The inspector suggested it might save time to hire a professional mason. "Hell, no," said the executive. "I'm going to
build this place myself. Every brick. Every stick."

"Plumbing too?" asked the inspector gloomily.

"Plumbing too."

"Electrical work?"

"You bet."

The inspector went away sadly. "I feel kind of sorry for
that guy," he told me later. "I know I'm going to have to make
him do everything twice before he gets it right. He's going to
hate me. It'll take him fifty years to build that house, if he
doesn't electrocute himself first."

But there was no need to feel sorry for the man. He wanted weekend work.

Work has long held the status of a religion in America. Perspiration has been a favorite subject of poetry. School children for almost a hundred years have been instructed to admire Longfellow's village blacksmith, whose brow was wet with honest sweat. Some have called it sweat, some have reached for euphemisms. Oliver Wendell Holmes once wrote a poem about a ploughman and referred reverently to "toil's bright dewdrops." No matter. It's still the same clammy stuff. And deeply embedded in our feelings is the idea that it is the stuff which makes us noble.

The gospel of work, so-called, has been hanging around the western world for a long time. It appeared in a specific and direct form in monasteries during the Dark Ages. Monks dedicated themselves to a life of toil, for toil was one of the means by which they thought to purify themselves. Work has always managed to get Heaven on its side. The gospel of work probably did a great deal in smoothing the debut of the industrial age. Management could suggest to the workers that toil was what they really wanted. In fact, management was doing them a favor by giving them so much of it. And a worker could use the gospel to rationalize meaning into his life if he felt it was otherwise meaningless. He could think: I may be miserable but by God I'm pure.

Work was lined up on the side of God, home, mother and morality. Its opposites were all the things that are suspected to be fun but are generally agreed to be poisonous, all the red and purple things like sloth, luxury and debauchery. Work is anti-sin. Work redeems us. Indeed a number of poems written in the nineteenth century come right out and say work is prayer, and half a dozen popular Protestant hymns make the same suggestion.

This idea proved handy in the settling and taming of America and was undoubtedly an important fuel for the enormous task. The early New Englanders were people of a pronouncedly sweat-worshiping persuasion. It was lucky they were. Without its strong religious tone their backbreaking dawn-to-dark work of survival in a wilderness might have overwhelmed them. The stern New Englanders shied away from thoughts of leisure. Possibly they were afraid they'd break down and weep if they let themselves reflect on what they were missing. They cast all such thoughts from their heads. Idleness was, if not in itself sin, at best a richly manured seedbed in which sin could sprout. The early settlers had their good times of course, but they constantly reminded themselves that these were just breaks in the only important activity—doing the Lord's work. They had to have these breaks because they were human and weak. They hoped the Lord would forgive them.

The union of work with righteousness helped keep our

ancestors content as they toiled their weary way into the West. It was with us as the industrial age arrived with its hateful clock. It was still with us as rising productivity began to cut down our requirements for work.

And where did this leave us? In a vacuum. Walter Kerr in *The Decline of Pleasure* puts it like this: "The Twentieth Century has relieved us of labor without at the same time relieving us of the conviction that only labor is meaningful." We feel lost and uncomfortable when our brows aren't wet with honest sweat. There are two days of this discomfort every week.

"Our whole culture is built on the ethic of work," says Dr. Alexander Reid Martin. "We have no heritage of leisure. We have no real basis for enjoying free time." We find it hard to think of any activity that is half as noble as work. The opinion polling company Elmo Roper & Associates once asked a sampling of weekenders what might happen if we were given a third workless day per week. Some 20 per cent predicted we'd get soft and lazy, and another 20 per cent thought we'd be bored stiff. These are ignoble concepts: softness, laziness and boredom. They invite visions of people lolling about like patricians in the twilight of the Roman Empire, bloated with rich food and wine, sated with orgy, soft of spine and empty of head. This is what work saves us from.

The psychoanalyst S. Ferenczi was intrigued by the relationship of men and women to their work. He coined the term "Sunday neurosis," Sunday at that time being the only ordinary day off. Psychiatrists still use the term in referring to the entire weekend. Ferenczi theorized that work is a kind of comfortable straitjacket. It keeps us in line. The sober atmosphere and narrow purposefulness of the ordinary workday provide "external censors" to hold us steady. These censors help cage in the urges toward sex, murder and mayhem which, in analytic theory, shriek and seethe within us. On weekends the external censors are removed. Then the internal censors must work all the harder. Ferenczi believed that many people do not trust their internal censors to hold. They're scared of free time because they're scared of what they might do in it.

A Detroit psychiatrist, Dr. Jean Rosenbaum, has spent several years making a study of holidays and their effects on people. "These effects are most noticeable around major holidays such as Christmas," he says, "but you can see them on an ordinary weekend too. A work-free day is an invitation to regress toward childhood a little, to obey our whims and impulses. This is a fine healthy thing but it has its frightening elements. For we have whims and impulses that aren't acceptable even in the relaxed mood of the weekend." A man may dream all week of raping his neighbor's wife, for instance. He easily holds the lid on the impulse with work's help. But on weekends he finds the urge boiling higher. Perhaps at a party he finds himself nearly out of control. It scares him. He scurries back to the safety of work.

And not only is work aligned with morality, but it moves toward definite goals—individual goals such as higher income and prestige, high-sounding goals such as the progress of the company and the defense of the nation. The weekend doesn't have tangible goals like these, unless you count goals that are related to work. Weekend recreation in general is supposed to tune us up so we can be efficient working machines again on Monday. This is the kind of reasoning favored by corporate recreation directors. It pulls the weekend down to the level of the workday morning coffee break—a chunk of leisure time designed to serve work.

The weekend's own goals are mostly impractical ones like happiness and the feel of good living. There are probably practical ones too, but they aren't obvious like those of work. For example, William James thought one purpose of play is to let us express instincts that are otherwise squashed in civilized life. He used the term "play" broadly, noting Friedrich von Schiller's theory that art is a mature form of play. But a week-

ender isn't likely to have this thought on the tip of his tongue when you accost him at a bowling alley and ask why he is rolling balls at sticks. He will probably mumble that bowling is fun and makes him happy. These reasons sound frivolous compared with reasons for working.

The weekender is rare who can articulate other than hazy reasons for his Saturday and Sunday activities. I met one such weekender a few years ago. His name was Will Yolen. He works for a publicity agency and spends his workdays in the high-pressure, three-Gibsons-for-lunch world of advertising and television. On weekends he flies kites. One day the editors of *True* Magazine called me in and said, "Listen, why the hell would a man fly kites?" I didn't know, so I went to see Will Yolen. He said, "You can look at that kite in the sky and think about big things. All the little things quit bothering you."

That seems like a good reason for playing—if you must have a reason. Must you? Play is pleasant. Isn't that enough? Unhappily, in our work-oriented society, it usually isn't.

Broadly speaking, there are two main classes of seven-day toilers. One class might be called the homogenizing toiler. His object is to homogenize the week so that all seven days are equally filled with the ennobling and meaningful requirements of his job. Perhaps it is not fair to say this is his object, for he may not consciously think of it that way. But at least it can be said this is his result. Saturday and Sunday are as nearly like Wednesday as he can make them.

The most obvious example of this class is the seventy-hour-a-week executive. Vance Packard in *The Pyramid Climbers* notes that the seventy-hour week is ordinary and expected among men scrambling for the top. *Fortune*'s Associate Editor Richard Whalen, reporting on the progress of a big manufacturing company in 1962, gave a particularly gloomy picture of the phenomenon: "The seven-day, 80-hour week of the frenetic early days is only slightly reduced now. The Saturday morning meeting is standard operating procedure. The company's executives travel and confer only on weekends."

I remember once trying to land an interview with a vice-president when I was a reporter on *Business Week*. I tried to hunt down the fellow at his office but nobody knew or would say where he was. Then I hit on the strategy of calling him at his home on Saturday. The lady who answered the phone seemed quite amused. "My goodness," she said, "this is the worst time to try to call him. Weekends are when he does his paperwork. He won't speak to anybody." When my sad farewell revealed my assumption that this lady was his wife, she laughed again. "I'm his secretary," she said.

It's not only top executives who are homogenizers, of course. All kinds of men and women, on all levels of the climb, practice this strange escape from freedom. So do housewives. The weekend finds the homogenizing housewife jittering about her home as desperately as she does all week. When her husband seeks out some quiet corner and settles into it with his newspaper, she is on the spot quickly, cracking his ankles with the vacuum cleaner. Or she is in the kitchen, loudly rattling crockery. She forbids him to relax. She makes plain her view that, since she is working, he should be too. When you ask her why she can't put off polishing the silverware until Monday, she speaks as though the household were some inexorably advancing glacier that will bury her if she doesn't chop at it every day. "It gets ahead of you," she says. She brushes a dangle of hair from her damp forehead.

Of course there could be reasons for such behavior other than the attempt to escape sin or futility. Some may be good reasons. But most of them go back to the view of work as the most significant and right thing in the world. For the sake of work a family will willingly pack up and move across the country.

Sadly the transferee and his wife say farewell to old friends and a beloved town. But they do not doubt they're doing the right thing. They don't feel obliged to explain their choice between home and work. Their friends would make the same choice. In *The Organization Man* William H. Whyte, Jr., quotes a busy young executive as saying he'll be relieved when his kids grow up. Then he won't feel guilty about neglecting them for his work. Evidently it hasn't occurred to him that he has a choice. He could neglect the work instead. But work worship goes so deep that it has the large solid feel of truth. Work is more important than family.

Small wonder there are so many homogenizers among us. How can the weekend offer any real value to one so bound to the work ethic?

Note something else about the homogenizer. Often he is a man, or woman, whose work gives him prestige. He's an executive or a member of the talent elite. From Monday to Friday he's a big man. People look up to him. Assistants and secretaries flutter about him. He and the United States Treasury share each payday in a nice round amount of the stockholders' money. Then Friday evening comes. Suddenly he is shorn of his work. He stands there naked and shivering. He is like a big beautiful bird whose feathers have come out. He plops to the ground and shambles morosely into the underbrush, a scrawny and most unprepossessing fowl.

His defense is the homogenizing technique. Carefully, carefully he saves up work to do over the weekend. He seeks out other men and women in the same predicament and arranges weekend meetings and trips with them. Possibly he doesn't realize what he is doing or why. He believes he must work over the weekend because there is so much work to do. He rationalizes that other men competing with him are also working seventy hours a week. On the surface these may seem like true pressures. But when probed, they disintegrate. In any large company you will find men working seventy hours, but you will

also find men working forty hours and apparently quite satisfied with their future prospects. Except possibly in the top
executive levels the seventy-hour week is usually the result of
individual choice, not imposed pressure. Parkinson's famous
law states that "Work expands to fill the time available." The
homogenizer simply makes all seven days available.

Consider an example from a psychiatrist's casebook. The
patient in this case was a man earning about $15,000 a year
and aiming higher. He was in rough shape. A perforated gastric
ulcer had almost killed him a few months before, and he was
developing another. He was a seventy-hour man. His wife was
threatening to leave him. He seldom spoke to her even on
weekends, and the only sexual intercourse they ever had was an
occasional hurried chore on Saturday night when he didn't
have to get up early the next morning.

The doctor was trying to find out what made the man work
so long. For half an hour the patient had stubbornly insisted he
had no choice. The five-day week didn't contain enough hours
for the work he had to do. If he hoped to get ahead, he had to
put in time on weekends. Finally the psychiatrist said, "All
right, let's look at this in detail. Take last Monday. Tell me
everything you did that day."

Patient: "Well, in the morning I had to fly to (a city some
two hundred miles away) to confer with some branch-office
people."

Doctor: "About what?"

Patient: "Oh, a question of sales. I wanted to get some
figures from them and ask their opinion about something."

Doctor: "Couldn't you have done this by mail or phone?"

The patient didn't think so at first. But after a while he
admitted the doctor might be right. He continued: "I got
back to the home office early in the afternoon and started to
dictate some letters. But then my boss called a meeting that
lasted till five."

Doctor: "Did you have to go to this meeting?"

Patient: "Oh, yes."

Doctor: "I mean, was attendance mandatory?"

Patient: "Well, no, not if you put it that way." In fact he admitted after more probing that the meeting hardly concerned his job area at all. He'd attended mainly "because things can slip past you if you don't keep watching." His diary continued: "I got a few letters out, then went to meet a customer and his wife who were visiting town. I had to take them to dinner and the theater."

Doctor: "Had to?"

Patient: "Oh, yes. It's SOP in my business. When a big spender comes to town you show him a good time."

Doctor: "Wouldn't it be almost as satisfactory just to give the customer the tickets? And maybe arrange his hotel reservations?"

The patient doubted it. But he agreed he could let colleagues and subordinates share the wining and dining of customers instead of always volunteering himself.

Doctor: "Do you realize something?"

Patient: "What?"

Doctor: "Everything you accomplished in that long day could have been done in an hour or two."

When the session ended, the patient was still arguing vehemently that the psychiatrist didn't understand the world of business. The patient was a homogenizer. He carefully expanded his work to fill a seven-day week. No doctor was going to expose him to the chill vacuum of workless weekends.

The homogenizer will go to great lengths to deny the existence of Saturday and Sunday. His attempt to bind himself to his work may have bizarre results. For instance, he may get involved in a rather weird type of love affair with a secretary or some other women about the plant or office. A New York psychoanalyst tells a typical story. The man, married and in his early forties, worked for a small electronics company where he had a responsible engineering post. In that small pond he was a large frog. In the neighborhood where he lived, he was a mere tadpole. Many of his neighbors had more glamorous jobs in bigger companies. What was just as unbearable, many were able to shine more brightly in the weekend society. On weekends the engineer felt demoted, drab and insignificant. Since his wife was always with him at these unhappy times, he associated her with them. He was sure she saw him as he felt, and maybe she did.

But with his secretary at the plant he was big and brilliant. Here was a young woman who had been with him as he fought heroic battles and scored great victories. She knew what kind of man he really was. Understandably, in time, he came to prefer her gaze to his wife's.

The first signs of trouble were the ordinary stigmata of the developing homogenizer. The engineer brought work home in his attaché case. On Friday nights he resisted the change of clothes that symbolizes a change of role. While his neighbors were appearing in sports clothes and their old Army fatigues, he kept his workday armor tightly buckled on. He began going to the plant on Saturday mornings to "clear his desk." On Sunday nights he went to bed even earlier in anticipation of dear Monday. When he began telling his wife to turn down Saturday night social engagements, his transformation into a homogenizer was just about complete.

Then he started to bring his secretary into the effort. Sometimes they'd work late Friday night, and he would take her out

to dinner. Occasionally he'd ask her to meet him Saturday
morning at the plant. It started innocently. But the engineer
noted how good he felt in the girl's presence. He didn't try to
figure out why. He thought it was love. He made a play for her,
and she responded. Perhaps she was a homogenizer too and, for
similar reasons, felt good in his presence. A full-scale office
romance was ignited.

It ended messily in divorce. And the sad thing was that it
was all founded on a disastrous mistake. The engineer thought
he was in love with his secretary. What he really loved was the
image of himself that he saw mirrored in her eyes.

The second type of seven-day toiler might be called the two-
stage, or variegating, toiler. This is the man or woman who
continues to work through the weekend but at a task or tasks
different from his Monday to Friday job. Normally he isn't
sorely troubled by the weekend loss of job prestige that afflicts
homogenizers. But his other aches and itches are common
among both kinds of seven-day toilers—and indeed among the
majority of us who have streaks of work worship in us.

He may tell you he needs more money. This is the reason
commonly given by the most conspicuous two-stager of all,
the double jobholder, or moonlighter. According to the Bureau of Labor Statistics there are about 3 million people in this
country with two or more jobs. Their number fluctuates between roughly 4 and 5 per cent of the employed population,
apparently depending on economic conditions and prospects.
The amount of moonlighting goes up in periods when there's
anxiety about layoffs, shutdowns and business failures. Undoubtedly some moonlighters are motivated by a real need for
money.

Some are motivated by desire, not need. Ironically a moonlighter often starts his weekendless career when he decides he
wants more leisure equipment. He tells himself: I'll hold this
second job just long enough to buy my Zoomo Cabin Cruiser,
Cadillac of the Waterways. Then I'll quit. That is what he tells
himself. He may actually believe it. But Parkinson's law could

probably be restated: "Expenses expand to consume the money available." Once a family gets used to a certain income level, a 25 per cent cut becomes a disaster. For one thing the very ownership of the coveted Zoomo creates new expenses by itself. I know a schoolteacher who joined a real-estate outfit as a weekend salesman to earn money for a backyard swimming pool. That was eight years ago. He is still selling real estate. He hears the pool is a great success with the neighborhood kids.

Other moonlighters lack even the explanation of a specific buy-dream. They speak of wanting more money in general. Of course, a few are battling economic catastrophes such as major hospital bills, but most can only tell you they want more income as a matter of principle. This explanation seldom sounds like the whole truth. The state of wanting more money is almost universal. I want more, you want more. But only some of us would trade our weekends for it.

Redbook Magazine once published an article by a young mother whose husband was a moonlighter. He was a solemn, playless man. His primary job earned quite enough for gracious living, yet he held a second job which used both weekend days and most nights. Why? His explanation, as his wife reported it, was that he felt the most worthwhile thing he could do was earn for his family. Noble enough. But it seems odd to go to the trouble of creating a family, then spend the rest of your waking life away from it, supplying it with goods.

No, the need-for-money explanation isn't always the real one. Often the truth is that the moonlighter can find no contentment outside his work. And the same can be said of the other kind of two-stager, the man or woman who creates his or her own unpaid work with which to keep busy on weekends.

It is hard to spot this kind of two-stager or to say definitely that this man or that woman is one. The do-it-yourself movement in this country is huge. The land is wet with the sweat of home gardeners. Millions of foot-pounds of energy are expended each weekend by work squads in churches, political clubs, PTA chapters and Scout troops. The reasons people have for doing all this work are many and various. The creative aspects of home carpentry and weekend farming are appealing to some. Others endure the work for the sake of the gracious setting they hope will result, or for reasons of community standing. Some join church groups for social reasons and accept the work as an unavoidable byproduct. To say all these people are work worshipers would be ridiculous.

But there are seven-day toilers among them. When Elmo Roper's pollers buttonholed a sample of weekenders and asked what they would do if given a third workless day, in addition to 25 per cent who said they'd get part-time jobs (potential moonlighters), 37 per cent said they'd use the extra time to work around the house and 5 per cent said they disliked the whole idea. This whole group probably represents a pretty heavy concentration of work worshipers. These are people who, when the work weekend was mentioned, reacted either by thinking of work or with revulsion, or both.

The unpaid two-stager is beaded with toil's bright dewdrops all weekend. Acquaintances secretly hate him because he's so damned efficient. The ashtrays in his car are empty and the clock is on time. He reads the care-and-maintenance booklets that come with pieces of equipment he buys and follows directions to the letter. He oils his wife's vacuum cleaner, puts new dust filters in his air conditioner and reverses the washers in his bathroom faucets. His Zoomo Cabin Cruiser, Cadillac of the Waterways, is a boundless source of delight to him. He had no interest in buying a boat until one day he went to a local marina and saw all the boat owners at work. He seldom takes his Zoomo out on the water, and when he does he spends the time tinkering with the motor. Mostly it sits in its berth or up on a cradle. He winterizes it, summerizes it, paints it, sands varnish off the decks, puts more varnish on so he can sand it off again, takes the motor apart, puts it back together and instantly becomes convinced it still isn't quite right. In spare moments he stands around and frowns at the Zoomo in a workmanlike way.

The suburban subphylum is perhaps even more conspicuous.

His garage and cellar are immaculate, earning the ill will of less
tidy neighbors whose spouses point to him as a good example.
He does all the jobs home-handyman magazines say you should
do but nobody else does. He caulks his window frames, paints
his wooden gutters with linseed oil, drains his water heater and
washes his garden tools after using them. He's likely to have
a bulletin board on which, through the week, he lists things to
do over the weekend. He encourages other family members to
add to the list. Sometimes he has a nightmare in which he goes
to the bulletin board Saturday morning and finds only a blank
sheet of paper. As with leisure equipment, he is repelled by
labor-saving devices until he sees they can be the source of new
labor. He was one of the last men on his block to buy a power
lawnmower, but now that he has one he takes it apart regularly
for cleaning and oiling, sharpens the blades at least once a
year and when winter comes, winterizes it. As a neighbor once
said of such a man: "He oils his door hinges, for God's sake."

The female of the species is equally resourceful in escaping
freedom. She, too, does all the jobs urged by experts. She paints
shelves before putting shelf paper on them. She paints the un-
dersides of chairs. She is likely to be a childherd. She teaches
Sunday school, sells refreshments at Little League games and
takes Girl Scouts to dairy farms. Other women volunteer or are
drafted as childherds on some weekends, but she signs up at
every opportunity. She makes the others feel guilty. She is proud
of her hard and righteous life. She sighs loudly when she sits
down. If you offer her a cup of coffee, she appears to fight a
battle with her conscience. "All right," she says finally, "but I
can only stay a little while." Then she tells you of the missions
on which she must so soon depart. In her wake you feel repre-
hensibly lazy.

Dr. Alexander Reid Martin is fond of remarking that there
are people who can relax only when a doctor orders them to.
Then worklessness becomes useful, a health matter. It can be
enjoyed or at least tolerated without feelings of guilt or futility.
If you catch a work worshiper in a rare moment of play and ask

him why, he is likely to speak in medical terms. You've got to have leisure or you'll tighten into a quivering tangle of nerves, your stomach will digest itself and your heart will explode. These are excellent reasons for seeking weekend relaxation. The work worshiper must have reasons. His spirit doesn't feel competent or worthy to sing for its own sake but must always have some clear hard goal outside itself.

Most of us find ourselves in the same trap at least some of the time. We've got to have reasons. We're troubled by what Dr. Martin calls "the conditional view of life." We have a feeling that happiness is given to us on condition that we deserve it or will turn it to some more lofty purpose. Nothing is free, not love and certainly not weekends. "The belief that leisure must be earned will die hard," Margaret Mead once remarked. Longfellow's notorious blacksmith couldn't lay down his tools until he had "earned a night's repose."

But this too makes the weekend an overgrown cousin of the workday coffee break, a reward for last week's work and a medicine for producing brightness of eye next Monday. It puts the weekend in a slavish relationship to the workweek. How can a weekender enjoy his free time wholeheartedly when he doesn't even respect it?

Perhaps one of the problems is that the weekend is shorter than the workweek and hence looks less significant. But in some of our lifetimes the weekend may expand to three or even three and one-half days.

A New York union recently wrested from its employers a 25-hour workweek. This was mainly a device for smoothing layoff procedures and gaining overtime pay, but it hauls down from the level of abstraction the idea of a weekend stretching across half the week. Will we know what to do with ourselves in such a weekend? Will we be able to use it to the fullest? What then? Somehow we've got to discover that leisure is as worthy as work. It doesn't have hard reasons, but it needs none. The only thing we need to know about happiness is that it makes us happy.

4. The Fun Mystique

At the Southern Hills Country Club in Tulsa, Oklahoma, there used to appear each Saturday morning a weekender whom the caddies called Old Vinegar. They called him other things, too. The odd thing about Old Vinegar was that he was said to be a reasonable man during the rest of the week. He was an executive of an oil company. Stories circulated about his goodness of heart. He'd given a subordinate money to pay hospital bills, for instance. He'd helped a secretary who found herself pregnant out of wedlock.

But on weekends he was possibly the most spectacularly nasty man west of the Mississippi. He hated caddies. He particularly hated the schoolboys who came up to the course to caddie on weekends. Thus the ordeal of carrying his bags always fell to us "regulars." We were a group of broke and jobless men who had been stranded in Tulsa by a recession. In this way I was given the opportunity to make my first detailed study of a weekender. I'd walk the fairways with Old Vinegar and wonder what had caused him. William Blake's irritating nonrhyme about the tiger kept rasping through my head. Old Vinegar, I would think, what immortal hand or eye could frame thy fearful symmetry? Sometimes I'd say it aloud in a futile attempt to make it rhyme better, and once I made the mistake of mum-

bling it when Old Vinegar was addressing his ball before a
difficult seven-iron shot.

"What's that?" he barked.

"I was reciting some poetry, sir," I said.

"Well, keep it to yourself. If there's any place in the world
where poetry doesn't belong, it's a damned golf course!"

Old Vinegar hated golf, but he played all weekend. He
played in blistering heat and howling rainstorms. He hated
weather of any kind, even sunshine, which got in his eyes. He
hated everybody in his foursomes, including himself. Sometimes
when his shot went wild, he'd tear off his cap and whack himself
on the head with it. And never was he heard to say a pleasant
word to a caddie. He hated caddies when they were in sight
because they made him nervous. He brooded about them when
they were out of sight because he thought they were helping
themselves from the bottle of Canadian he kept in his bag. As
a matter of fact, they were. It was a custom of long standing for
caddies to be the golfers' guests on cold days, when they were
hidden around a dogleg or behind a high green. Most of the
golfers accepted the situation with gloomy humor. Old Vinegar
made a federal case out of it.

Old Vinegar's wife was a sweet, amiable woman. On weekends she liked to be surrounded by gaiety, and it bothered her
that Old Vinegar always looked so dyspeptic. Often she would
be found waiting for him as he grumped his way up to the
eighteenth green. To make him smile she'd offer meek little
jokes, asking, for example, whether it was against the club
bylaws for golfers to be happy.

My last memory of Old Vinegar is a picture of him facing
his wife after one such gentle prodding. His face was red with
sunburn and rage. He looked as though he were about to burst
into tears.

"I'm happy!" he roared. "God damn it, can't you understand
I'm happy?"

That was many years ago. The recession ended and I left

Tulsa to seek my fortune elsewhere. I never saw Old Vinegar again. But in 1962 I heard a story about a weekender at the Arundel Golf Club at Kennebunkport, Maine. I like to think this weekender was Old Vinegar. In fact my sense of artistic wholeness insists that it was. The story was reported gleefully by the Associated Press, which seldom misses a chance to rib golfers. It is a lovely sad story of death and redemption.

Here is the story. I title it Old Vinegar at Kennebunkport. Onlookers watched one Sunday while he knocked several balls into a stream, his wrath mounting with each dismal plop. As his last ball disappeared from sight, he apparently reached the final decision. He seized his bag of clubs and hurled them into the water. Luckily he had no caddie at the time, for the next thing into the water was his caddie cart. He then sat down, took off his cleated golf shoes and heaved them to oblivion after the cart.

The onlookers by this time were worked up to a climax of tragic appreciation. Imagine their terrible disappointment when Old Vinegar, having begun to stride away, paused and seemed to waver with indecision. Forlorn anticlimax! He walked back to the stream, waded in and pulled his golf bag back from the depths. No, no!

No. He unzipped the ball pocket, pulled out his car keys, carefully rezipped the pocket and hurled the bag into deeper water. Then he waded out of the stream, strode soggily across the fairway and disappeared into the sunset.

Probably it wasn't the game of golf specifically that soured Old Vinegar's temper. Golf is like any other game. Some enjoy it, some don't. Old Vinegar didn't. Yet some demon hounded him along the fairways when he would rather have been at home with a book or scrabbling in his vegetable patch.

What demon was this? The same one that hounds the majority of weekenders—a belief in the absolute necessity of fun. Fun might be called the active youthful part of good living. In the weekend society, which worships youth, to be funless is to invite scorn and pity. Anybody without fun is felt to be a failure in the art of living.

The weekender feels required to be as successful at play as at work. He must have fun in such a way that everybody knows he is having fun, even if he isn't. This is what goaded Old Vinegar bellowing down the fairways. He wanted to show he was a well-rounded fellow, capable of enjoying himself. He didn't want people pointing to him and saying, "Poor man, he just doesn't know how to *live.*"

The feeling that one ought to have fun exists in direct contradiction to the much older puritan or work ethic. It is superimposed on top of the older feeling like a coat of iridescent paint. The two feelings exist in the weekender simultaneously. Sometimes one gains supremacy, sometimes the other. Each causes trouble in its own way. The two together cause the most painful kind of conflict.

The fun mystique became a national weekend phenomenon some time in the 1940's. One of the first to recognize it was Martha Wolfenstein, psychology professor at Yale University's Child Study Center. Studying movies as a social symptom with her husband, Nathan Leites, she became aware that a new type of heroine had become popular. This was the fun girl. Her main attraction was not sex, brains, moral character or any of the older attributes that once drew people to the screen. Her charm was in her capacity to make fun easy for her companions, usually male. She could have and cause fun anywhere—a park bench, a hot dog stand, a shabby apartment. With her around nobody need work hard to have fun.

Dr. Wolfenstein went on thinking about this girl and what she represented. People apparently felt socially pressured to have fun, or to give the outward appearance of it. As a result fun was often an onerous chore instead of—well, fun. How long had this odd compulsion been with us? Was there a way to pin it down and analyze it?

Dr. Wolfenstein reasoned that adult feelings about fun are

reflected in theories on bringing up children. Thus a study of changing fashions in child psychology through the years ought to give some index of changing attitudes toward work and play. Out of this came Dr. Wolfenstein's classic essay, "The Emergence of Fun Morality," which appeared in 1951 in the *Journal of Social Issues.*

Fashions in child psychology are faithfully reflected in the bulletin *Infant Care,* published by the Children's Bureau of the U.S. Department of Labor. This was Dr. Wolfenstein's source of clues. The bulletin was first published in 1914. In those early years it warned parents that they were in a grim battle with their child's base impulses. If they didn't firmly hold him in line, his sinful, pleasure-seeking nature would get the best of them and ruin him. If he was crying in hunger or pain it was all right to pick him up, but if he only wanted affection or other merely pleasurable things the parents must sternly leave him crying in his crib. The mother was warned not to play with him too much. This led to unhealthy excitement and was bad for his nerves. Fun was not only purposeless but associated with sin and nervous decay. These are precisely the terms of the work ethic.

By the mid-1940's Dr. Wolfenstein finds the bulletin completely revised. Now fun is not only allowed, but required. The baby needs play as much as he needs food. The parents shouldn't worry about his thumb sucking and other habits. He's just growing up. Where the 1914 mother was praised for "wisdom," "strength" and "patience," the whole parenthood experience in 1945 is portrayed as a kind of sincere lark. "The parents are promised that having children will keep them together, keep them young and give them fun and happiness."

By the early 1950's some nagging doubts slithered into this happy land. What weekenders had discovered years before—that it isn't easy to have fun on demand—is now applied to the baby. He might not automatically have fun in his bath.

His mother must think of ways to make it fun. What's more, the work ethic can once more be seen lurking in the shadows. The bulletin now counsels the mother not to pick up the baby *every* times he cries. They warn her she must control him. There is still a fear of uncontrolled pleasure seeking.

The modern mother clearly has a harder task than the mother of 1914. Today's mother lives on a rack, pulled by opposing ethics. Should she be strict or permissive? Is the youngster her opponent or junior partner? This conflict is painful enough in itself. But far more painful at times is the requirement that the mother herself have fun. If she doesn't have fun with her baby, she must suspect she isn't a good mother or even a whole woman. As Dr. Wolfenstein puts it, "Her self-evaluation can no longer be based entirely on whether she is doing the right and necessary things, but becomes involved with nuances of feeling which are not under voluntary control."

And so it is with the weekender. His self-esteem and prestige depend on his success in having, or at least demonstrating, fun.

Where did the fun mystique come from? One source was probably a reaction to the grimness and greyness of the work ethic. People must have grown tired of having their pleasures spoiled by the feeling that pleasure was frivolous or wrong. They reacted with a declaration of principles opposite to those of the work ethic. Homespun, or speakeasy, philosophers in the 1920's were already beginning to insist that fun is important. What good is life without it? Let yourself go! All this sounded wise, pleasantly rebellious and titillatingly spiced with sin. In time it became social dogma.

Sigmund Freud also contributed. Sociologist Richard La-Piere in *The Freudian Ethic* calls the master analyst's teachings "a doctrine of social irresponsibility." There are many who would argue that Freudian ideas aren't that bad, or at least that their effects haven't gone that deep in most people. But there is no doubt Freud's teachings or the distortions of them,

which have widely permeated our society, lend a kind of authoritative blessing to the idea of letting go. One should not be inhibited. The weekend should be a period in which we wriggle out of the workweek's harness and whoop it up. Cavort! Sport! Sin! These are the wise and sophisticated things to do.

Weekenders do them in a variety of ways, most of which lead to exhaustion. Among the most visible kinds of fun is the warm-weather pilgrimage to water. The Bureau of Public Roads says passenger cars in this country traveled nearly 600-billion miles in 1960, three times as far as in 1945. Much of this fantastic distance was covered by weekenders visiting sea beaches, lakes and other water resorts. A psychoanalyst once theorized that people are drawn to water because it reminds them of the womb. The object might be achieved by immersing oneself in a bathtub. But a bathtub doesn't provide visible fun. And despite the recent proliferation of backyard swimming pools a widely accepted standard is that the weekender's water fun may be measured at least partly by the distance he drives to find it.

One reason for this is that metropolitan weekenders dream of finding lonely beaches. The ideal beach for which the week-ender hunts eternally is one with no more than one bathing party every fifty yards, where the only sounds are the scattered cries of people having fun graciously and the mournful calls of a few select waterfowl. There are of course few such beaches left within weekend distance of any major metropolitan area. Almost all accessible beaches are thickly populated with teen-agers playing transistor radios and small boys, roughly six years old, who wander the sands carrying ice cream things on sticks and looking for people to trip over. David Boroff in *Harper's* a few years ago said of the Jewish resort area in the Catskills: "Though God made the country, man . . . can remake it in the image of the city." After driving three hours to escape the metropolitan crowds, the weekender discovers the crowds have followed the same route to escape him.

He knows this will always be so, yet weekend after weekend finds him taking to the road. He seeks distant water even though he has just bought a swimming pool, even though he belongs to a country club with a pool, even though his town or city has a fine beach of its own. He listens carefully to friends who have found a secret new route to this or that water resort, but on the day he tries it he finds the knowledge has been broadcast as though on nationwide TV. Small wonder there are twice as many automobile accidents on Saturdays as on weekdays. After an hour or two in irritable cheek-to-cheek traffic he begins to wonder if the good life is worth seeking after all. Children in the car will make him wonder all the harder. As regularly as metronomes they ask how much longer the trip will take, constantly reminding their parents of the vast hot distances yet to cover. All children store fluids with great care so that their bladders become unbearably full when the car is stopped in dead traffic miles from any service station, tree or bush. When we were kids, my father, to afford himself peace of mind, cut a trapdoor over the driveshaft. But cars today don't have plywood floors.

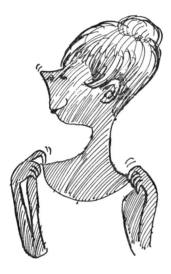

The trip may be so harrowing that the weekender, once arrived at the beach, spends much of his time there worrying about the trip home. He gazes thoughtfully over the vista of water, sand, empty beer cans, crumpled tubes of suntan lotion and discarded sunglass frames and wonders whether the living might really have been better back at the local swimming pool. But he gets his reward on Sunday night, after he has returned home. Some friends drop in for a gin and tonic. "We had a quiet weekend," they tell him. "Didn't go anywhere. Had a swim at the pool this afternoon, that's about all."

They look considerably more rested than he. They are not aflame with sunburn, nor are their muscles fused into the contours of an automobile seat. But our man now has his moment of glory. "Well," he announces, "we went to Hoohaw Lake." He has scored his point. Once again he has successfully had fun.

The weekenders also consider that outdoor eating provides a gracious kind of fun, whether or not performed at a beach. They go picnicking or, in the case of suburbanites, backyard barbecueing. They maintain food eaten outdoors tastes better. It is true that charcoal smoke imparts a special flavor to meats and fish, and a hamburger that has come apart, fallen through the grill and been grubbed out of the ashes has a flavor all its own. The pieces of charcoal and flakes of newspaper ash add a certain something. But the main reason why weekenders like cookouts is probably that, being metropolitans of largely indoor habit, they are attracted by the weekend ideal of outdoorness. They feel healthier after a picnic or barbecue than after an ordinary workweek meal.

Perhaps the muscular exertion involved adds to the feeling. Food, utensils and other equipment must be removed from the weekender's efficient step-saving kitchen and transported at a cost of many steps to the picnic or barbecue site, nightmarish in its inefficiency. In the old days a woman thus leaving her kitchen could be consoled by the thought that, whatever extra work a picnic might cause, at least she wouldn't have the kitchen to clean up later. But those were the days when we went picnicking with sandwiches, a bag of apples and a jug of milk. Among weekenders today the old ideal of outdoor simplicity, while it exists in an abstract kind of way, has virtually disappeared on the practical level. The ideal of gracious living has shoved it aside. Gracious living implies abundance and a gourmet style of eating. A cookout today requires barbecue sauce, one or more kinds of salad, coffee, lemonade or Fizzies, pickles, ketchup, mustard and ice cream. The kitchen is likely to end the day in worse disarray than would be the case after an indoor meal.

Among married couples it is normally the wife who packs the picnic basket or carries the food and equipment out to the barbecue pit. Single girls often get their men friends to help pack the basket. But it is almost always the man who lights the fire. There is something about lighting an outdoor fire that reassures metropolitan man of his manhood. Charcoal can be started by soaking it with gasoline or special preparations available at gracious-living stores, but many weekenders still prefer newspaper and kindling wood. Some even scorn newspaper and start with a little mound of twigs. This is the way real outdoorsmen used to do it in the northwoods or out on the prairies. Boy Scouts are said to be able to do it. The weekend fire lighter prides himself on using only one match. If the fire goes out he is seized with shame, and it is unkind to poke fun at him. He has failed to prove something about himself that he quite desperately wants to prove.

In cold weather the weekenders make pilgrimages to skating lakes and, more and more often in recent years, to ski resorts. Anybody who can tell friends on Monday that he has been to Sugarbush or Alpine Meadows or Aspen wins enough fun points to last him several weekends. In the early 1950's there were fewer than a million skiers in this country, but now the number is estimated at some three million and may never stop growing.

Generally speaking a ski weekend isn't likely to include young children. Married couples who head for the slopes Friday night normally leave their younger kids home. This is partly because skiing is felt to be too hard a sport for youngsters, though actually they're likely to get the hang of it much faster than grownups. But the main reason is that a ski weekend is often a social occasion for the adults.

College boys and girls particularly go to ski resorts to meet and be met. In fact some go without skis and with no intention of skiing. They go by bus and train when they can, for if they're lucky they'll have picked up a whole year's worth of dates before they even see any snow. Young and somewhat older

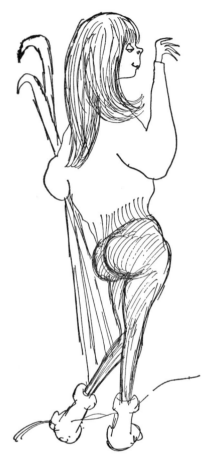

marrieds also go for reasons other than skiing. The mere act of leaving town with skis racked on top of one's car scores points. So does the fact of owning and sometimes wearing ski fashions, particularly stretch pants. "Millions of college girls look pretty in stretchies," a young mother remarked after a weekend at Stowe. "That's no great accomplishment. But you've no idea what it does to my morale each year when I find I can still wriggle into them. You know?"

The question of morale at ski resorts is a touchy one. There are few other sports in which experts have so haughty a disdain for duffers. Society around the slopes is stratified, not only according to wealth but also according to skiing proficiency. In the college crowd a girl who skis well won't normally date a clod who doesn't unless he is her only suitor at the moment.

Among adults the good skiers stick together in the lodges, bars and restaurants. Their clique is closed to beginners. The good-skiers' crowd is the high-fun crowd. Their success in skiing indicates they have had a lot of practice, which in turn indicates they are fun-every-weekend people. The feeling is that they are therefore successful at fun in general, including nighttime sociability. Everybody wants to join their elite group.

This creates problems, especially for ordinary weekenders

who lack time or money to get to the slopes often. A choice must be faced. You can go out on the slopes and practice in the hope of becoming proficient in a few years' time. But as you gyrate crazily downhill and plunge head first into the snow, you will automatically assign yourself to the bottom social stratum. You are a "plow," the lowest form of snow-borne life. Should you pause to meditate there awhile before pulling your head from the cool darkness, you may reflect that this is your only ski weekend this year, and isn't it a shame to spend so much money only to land at the bottom of a pecking order?

To avoid such a fate, you may choose not to ski at all. You hang around the lodge in your parka and square-toed boots, acting as though you just don't happen to feel like exerting yourself that day. Every time some plow wraps himself around a pine tree or tunnels into a drift on his elbows, you adopt the expression of one politely trying to suppress an amused smile. This ruse may win you acceptance in the high-fun crowd, or at least will prevent automatic rejection. But the trouble is that you never learn to ski this way. Nightmares will haunt you in which the high-fun crowd decides to go skiing and you can't think of a plausible excuse. The last that is heard of you is a hoarse quavering cry as you whirl helicopterlike off the edge of a precipice.

Maybe all this is fun and the weekender sometimes finds in it the aura of good living he seeks. Ski resorts in their brochures invariably show at least one picture of a group of gloriously healthy, immoderately attractive people relaxing around a roaring fire with Tom-and-Jerries. This looks like the good life, indeed. But often the weekender is too tense and tired to fit into the picture. What the brochure doesn't show is that these are clocked people. With only two days to find good living, they work at it too hard and worry about it too much.

The very intensity of the search dooms it to frequent failure. The weekender must find fun this weekend, not next. He's got to find it or face the pity of his neighbors who are really living.

He can't simply relax and let joy drift into his life at its own pace and in its own unpredictable way. He must go out and hunt it, corner it, chase it as it dodges again so nimbly from his grasp. But joy seems to be like a piece of soap. When you grab too fast and hard, it slips away.

Dr. Alexander Reid Martin likes to make a point about this. "There are some people," he says, "who achieve a leisurely state of mind for the first time in their lives when they miss a train and have an hour to kill before the next one." Here is an unplanned hour, dropped from heaven. Social pressures are absent. Unlike the weekender, the misser of train or plane is under no obligation to go out and have fun. He can simply sit and look at the clouds if he likes. He can amble about aimlessly. He can find a paper clip in his pocket and bend it into appealing shapes. He can browse in a bookstore. And thus, when under no kind of pressure to find any part of the good life, he may at last find it. He is a man completely at peace.

Here is a curious fact about our society. It is acceptable to sit doing nothing or to wander aimlessly around a transportation terminal. A man so occupied arouses no comment. He's obviously waiting with a reason. To a lesser extent the same behavior is all right in city office neighborhoods, too, at least on weekdays. The loiterer can be assumed to be killing time after lunch or before an appointment. But if you want to loiter around residential streets on a weekend, particularly in the suburbs, you should have with you either a dog, a child or a baby carriage—that is, a visible purpose. Otherwise you will be eyed with suspicion. You may even be stopped by a police prowl car. When you tell the cop you are just walking, he won't believe you. Nobody just walks. Even sitting on a park bench on weekends will mark you as odd.

Such is the pressure of the fun mystique. A weekender who does not at least sometimes pursue the accepted, youthful, visibly fun-filled enjoyments is thought not only unhappy and unsuccessful but also a bit weird. People suspect he ought to see a psychiatrist. Imagine what would happen if, say, Lewis Carroll were reincarnated in our age. His favorite Sunday sport was taking schoolgirls for long walks or boat rides and telling them stories. He'd sometimes go up to near strangers and say, "Madam, I am charmed by your little daughter. May I take her for a picnic with me on Sunday?" This was the gentle mathematician's way of having fun. But if he tried it today among the weekenders, he'd be considered strange and perhaps worse.

No, only certain activities are acceptable. The weekender likes to be thought of as an extrovert who lives in a loud fast whirl of activities and people. Anything less is felt to be almost if not quite pathological. The metamorphosis of boating in this country is an example. Boating used to be a quiet, rather solitary enjoyment. Most boat users were men. As portrayed on wall calendars and in ads for pipe tobacco, the typical boater spent his weekends alone or with a single friend (male) fishing on a lake surrounded by wilderness.

This was the situation in the 1940's. Then the fun mystique began to take over. Boating became more sociable, rowdier and younger at heart. People bought bigger boats that would hold bigger fun crowds. The average horsepower of all motors sold in 1947 was 4.7. In 1961 it was more than six times as much: 29.9. The bigger motors were preferred, not only because they had to power bigger boats but because they had to power more fun. There seemed to be a feeling that the horsepower of a weekender's motor reflected his frolic capacity. Big motor, big fun. The solitary pipe-smoking fisherman was no longer typical. With the pleased cooperation of boat and motor manufacturers, the picture was changed to that of a gay modern family and friends, their hair streaming in the wind, their faces radiant with barely containable delight.

Many boat owners do get joy from their sport. Others have been pressured into it. A psychiatrist told me a story about such a family. The family wanted to remodel itself in the young-at-heart image. Husband and wife wanted to get in with the gay crowd that thundered about a nearby lake on summer weekends. So they bought a boat.

Actually neither of them liked water sports much. Payments on the boat sucked the lifeblood from the family budget. The husband detested the chores of boat ownership: cleaning, painting, wintering. The wife spent her water-borne hours in an agony of fear that one of the kids would fall overboard and drown. Man and wife hated the boat but wouldn't admit it. In the end, nervously and inexpertly handled, the boat rammed into an obstruction, capsized and sank. Soggy but wiser, the two weekenders have since turned to other avenues in their pursuit of fun.

It isn't enough that fun be high-horsepowered. The weekender feels it ought to be varied too. This springs largely from the ideal of well-roundedness, the dream of a rich full life through which the narrowly specialized metropolitan can broaden himself on weekends. The weekender wants to sample many kinds of fun. His aim seems laudable, but he goes at it so hard that he often defeats himself. If he could content himself with one or two enjoyments on any given weekend, he could more often escape the curse of clockedness. But after an hour or two with his boat he must hurry home for a game of tennis. Then he must put in an appearance at a church fair, then home to greet some friends whom he has invited for drinks, then out again to play bridge. Dr. James A. Wylie of Boston University studied family recreation and found that the typical family has twenty to thirty different activities to keep it busy on weekends. Some have as many as seventy.

Our society in the past fifteen years has often been accused of succumbing to a disease called "spectatoritis." We've been pictured as sitting in stadia and before TV screens while our minds and bodies slowly flattened downward like lumps of lukewarm oatmeal. However, this picture has small basis in fact. The typical weekend is frantic, not lethargic. Dr. Alfred Clarke of Ohio State University demonstrated this in a 1956 study of free-time activity. Among people in the lowest job-prestige level, he found that only 24 per cent spend most of their workless time in the role of spectator; and in the highest level, only 26 per cent.

The same fact emerged from a Roper study of television's effects on free time. It might be expected that people with TV sets would leave the house for fun less often than those without. Not so. The Roper study showed virtually no difference between the two groups in their fondness for "going out." No, the role of spectator isn't a youthful or intense enough kind of fun. A family in its TV room or at a movie on Saturday afternoon or Saturday night feels faintly ashamed and considerably left out. One of the most telling weekend boasts is that of never having seen *Gunsmoke*.

The frantic weekend grows more so as you go upward through the educational, economic and job-prestige levels. A worried movie company once asked the Roper organization to find out why people were staying away from the big screen in such impressive numbers. The answer "Just too busy" was given by 15 per cent of people in the lower income group and 27 per cent in the upper. It was given by 17 per cent of high school graduates and 25 per cent of college graduates. In another Roper study for *Fortune*, people of various educational strata were asked what weekend activities they most enjoyed. The college graduates consistently named more activities than the high school graduates, who consistently named more than those who hadn't reach ninth grade. College graduates socialize more, play cards more, watch and participate in sports more, dabble more in arts and crafts, play and listen to music more. Only two things on this particular list were more popular among noncollege people: watching movies and doing needlework.

Much of this is explainable in terms of ordinary educational dogma. Education broadens the horizons, introduces a man or woman to sources of enjoyment that might otherwise have been ignored. But it also seems likely that college people are more sensitive to the pressures of the fun mystique. They are more likely to be pushed and pulled by the other-directedness that David Riesman identified in *The Lonely Crowd.* They've been bred to be sensitive to what others think, to shape each act and word for its effect on other people.

The Roper-*Fortune* study provides more evidence that this is so. At the bottom of the statistical summary is a category called "Don't know / No answer," referring to people who could only shake their heads when asked what weekend activities they enjoyed. Among those who had gone no further than ninth grade, almost 7 per cent were willing to see themselves put in this category. Among high school people the figure was 4 per cent. College people didn't want to admit even to a stranger that they lacked clear ideas about fun. Only 2 per cent of them failed to give some kind of answer.

The fear of being thought funless is one of the pressures that drive college people into aggressively high-fun sports like skiing and make them try so hard to be championship material. Some years ago a ladies' tennis instructor in the environs of Chicago averred in public that she preferred to teach women who were college graduates. She said they went at it in a more determined way than nongraduates. Her theory was that many college women had built grandiose career dreams in earlier life, had failed to achieve what they wished and now sought a substitute success on the tennis court.

This was a rather ill-considered statement for a tennis instructor to make publicly. It stirred up a storm of protests from both college and noncollege women. Yet what she said is echoed in private by other weekend counselors. Asked who enjoyed the sport more, a bowling instructor replied: "When they're beginners the noncollege people often seem to have a better time. They aren't so embarrassed about being beginners.

But when they get good the college folks are a lot louder about it. They enjoy it in a fiercer kind of way."

The very existence of weekend counselors and the fact that they make a living, often a good one, are direct results of the pressure to have fun successfully. Weekenders pay to learn golf, skating, skiing, bridge, arts and crafts and innumerable other types of fun. They also flock to various kinds of counselors who dispense advice and instruction without fee. For example, liquor dealers explain which wines go with which meats and suggest new drinking sophistications like putting radishes in Bloody Marys, to make the weekend seem high-fun.

Europeans visiting this country ten years ago used to express amazement at all this weekend counseling. "Must you be taught how to enjoy yourselves?" they asked nastily. Today of course Europe's prosperous economies probably support as many fun teachers per square mile as the United States does. You can get ping-pong lessons in France and hire a darts instructor in England.

The mere having of fun is not the whole battle, of course. While he is having it or when he has had it, the weekender must make sure other weekenders know about it. From the viewpoint of weekend prestige it would do him little good to frolic in secret. He seeks the inner sense of successful fun, but he also seeks the appearance of it.

An illuminating experience is to post yourself at some spot where the weekenders gather on Mondays—commuter train, coffee shop, supermarket or office water cooler—and listen to the conversations. Here are the weekenders practicing the difficult art of bragging by indirection. "At a party Saturday night I was talking to a fellow who. . . ." There is an excellent brag. While seeming to focus attention on the fellow who. . . , the weekender has adroitly given out the information that he went to a party. "Oh boy, I'm tired," groans another. "Don't seem to get much rest on weekends any more." Not subtle but competent. The weekender can let it go at that or supply details. Under the guise of complaint he can describe the concentrated fun that has so fatigued him.

Perhaps the best brag is a suntan. The brownish skin tone suggests hours of fun have been had on water, snow or fairway. Actually all that may have been had is acute discomfort in a fly-infested backyard, on a simmering rooftop or in the weird greenish glow of a sunlamp.

Even sports injuries can be used for the purpose. One of the most common skiing injuries is a broken or dislocated ankle, and this results in a highly visible plaster cast about the leg and foot. Skiers carrying this flamboyant badge take care to demonstrate that they didn't sustain the injury in any funless fashion such as falling downstairs, tripping over their shoelaces or catching their heels in sidewalk gratings. A skier in a cast walks the streets in his ski sweater (usually white, with red and green pine trees) and often in ski pants too. If on Monday he is forced to change into business clothes, he resorts to other advertisements. In Washington, D.C., a secretary at the Interior Department clumped about the halls for several weeks with a cast bearing the legend, "Courtesy of Sugarbush," in big red letters. On a commuter train once I saw a man who, to indicate the reason for his crutches, wore ski mittens, cap and parka with his natty dark blue suit.

Injuries are common among weekend athletes. Their way of life invites trouble. The medical profession hasn't reached real agreement on how much or what kind of exercise best suits those who lead the nonmuscular life of metropolia. All agree we'd be healthier if we had hard exercise daily, tapering off with age, but this is advice almost nobody takes. The typical weekender's life is frantic but not muscularly strenuous. We rush about in cars. We get winded emotionally but not physically. Faced with this, doctors aren't quite sure what to advise. But the majority opinion seems to be that anybody up to late middle age in normal health, leading an otherwise sedentary life, can play strenuous sports on weekends without harm and maybe with benefit—provided he does it every weekend. The man or woman who courts danger is the irregular weekend athlete, who goes several weeks without exercise and then suddenly taxes his body to the limit.

A body so taxed may be hurt. The surprised heart strains under a workload it isn't used to handling. Weak muscles in vulnerable places such as the lower back groan against their moorings. Tricky joints such as the ankles and knees, no longer strong enough to take the punishment, perform unreliably and may be damaged.

The results can be seen among weekenders everywhere on Mondays. The U. S. Public Health Service estimates that, not counting auto accidents or injuries on the job, some 32-million people in this country each year are hurt badly enough to require the attention of a doctor. In 1961, according to the National Safety Council, 18,400 people died from falls and 6,550 by drowning. There are also severe medical problems that may be precipitated or aggravated by overtaxing a soft body. In 1920 the death rate from heart ailments in this country was 163 per 100,000 people per year. In 1960 it was 366.

Among the most common Monday morning sights of medical interest is that of a weekender walking as though held together at the joints by sewing thread, which he fears will snap and cause him to disintegrate should he move too suddenly. This is a case of weekend back. The symptom is an acute pain in the lower back which makes sitting, standing and walking each more uncomfortable than the other two put together.

The Upjohn Company made a 12-year study of lower back pain among its employees and found that the ailment is most commonly caused by deep bending or twisting of the body without adequate warmup. Forty-nine per cent of the cases occurred in the first two hours of the morning and another eleven per cent in the first hour after lunch. This is why serious athletes warm up before starting strenuous activity. But weekenders never have time to warm up.

Yet in spite of himself and other obstacles the weekender sometimes tracks down and clutches to his heart the elusive feeling of fun. Only sometimes. His search is too frantic, busy and worried for it to be more than sometimes. Still it can't be said his quest is a total failure. It is just successful enough to keep him from losing interest.

As an emotion fun probably comes in at least as many varieties as there are people on earth. But broadly speaking it might be called a boisterous kind of happiness. It is not the happiness that steals over us, unexpected, in some lonesome twilight hour. It isn't the fierce glorious emotion that comes when we learn we've won a promotion or done in a rival. Nor is it the bland self-satisfied feeling we have as we view our newborn infant in the hospital, before we are responsible for changing his diapers. It is a big floating emotion, not perceivably connected with anything that can be talked about logically. Perhaps this is why it is so hard to summon up at will.

But there come moments when the weekender knows he has found it. He is gliding across a frozen lake on a winter afternoon. He is mad with spring and starlight at an outdoor supper. He is racing down a beach toward water. At moments like these he wishes the weekend could last a hundred years. It is sad that these moments don't come more often.

5. The People-liking People

THEY ARE CLEVER on Madison Avenue. They sense the moods of the times and aim their mercantile shafts at these moods. Here is a shaft that hit its mark. It is a television commercial urging us to buy a certain brand of bath soap. It shows a group of people gathered on some gay sociable occasion. Amongst them moves the hero or heroine of the story, bright, serene, feeding on the others' affections like a bee sipping nectar. "She likes people!" the accompanying ditty exults. "People like her!"

The weekender yearns to be with people-liking people. He wants to bathe all weekend in the invigorating surf of mutual popularity. He wants his ability to get along with people and their ability to get along with him to be demonstrated over and over again both to his inner self (probably most important) and to onlookers. He craves sociability.

He goes to card parties where sociability is mixed with bridge, to church parties where it is mixed with religion and to cocktail parties where it is served straight.

"God, how I hate these big weekend drinking parties," said a pretty young woman in New York, meditatively chewing an olive. "They're so unnatural." Like many Manhattan girls she pretended to have been reared on a farm in Kansas and to see earthy truths behind the metropolitan glitter. "All a cocktail party is," she said, "is an arena where everybody can bounce himself off everybody else and test how they react to him." Asked why she continued to go to parties, she thought for a while and said, "Well, actually, there's no sense spending Saturday night by yourself."

Of course not. The weekend is the time when you probe to see how much people really like you. During the week they are forced to be with you and be nice to you because their work requires it. On weekends you test their love for you in the abstract. A man once tried to sell the Mutual Broadcasting System a radio series called "Sounds of the Century," or something like that, and one of the sounds was a tape recording made secretly at a Saturday night alcohol feast. Above the din of mostly unintelligible talk a man's voice near the recorder could be heard exulting: "Everybody loves me and I love them, love them, love them . . . O God, I need another drink." Another man's voice fades in from the rumbling distance: "Say, anybody know where the bathroom is?"

The weekender who is searching for love is a determined joiner. He joins anything that offers him the promise of weekend companionship. He joins political clubs, glee clubs, bird-watching societies and groups devoted to the reading aloud of Gertrude Stein. He is behind the remarkable rise of church membership in the past fifteen years. He may belong to the Elks, Lions, Kiwanis or American Legion. Typically, if he is a parent, he belongs to children's service organizations which he has channeled into his own purposes of weekend sociability. He goes to PTA bazaars, Scout award dinners and 4-H picnics.

Or perhaps his son plays Little League baseball. Boys have great fun in this excellent outfit while their parents socialize. The Little League's official rules expressly forbid smoking around the benches or dugouts, but since it is rather hard for tobacco-addicted sociables to socialize without smoking, the rule is almost universally disregarded. Even the umpires smoke. So many people-liking people collect around the dugouts that team managers sometime have trouble locating their players.

Evidently it never occurred to the Little League's founders that their noble idea would be taken over by adult weekenders, for there is nothing in the rulebook about alcohol. Weekenders sometimes show up at Saturday-afternoon games with cans of beer or jugs of martinis. They hold an outdoor popularity exchange while the kids play. All this is probably quite harmless unless, as occasionally happens, the adult gathering overshadows the boys and their ball game. I recall umpiring at a game when a howl of laughter from the bleachers chanced to coincide with a ludicrous strikeout by a small, bespectacled batter. The boy thought they were laughing at him and ran off the field weeping.

If the weekender can afford it, he may belong to two or more

sociability clubs. The upper-middle weekender has his college
or downtown club in the heart of metropolia and his country
club out in the suburbs or the rural fringe. In the two increasingly metropolitanized decades since World War II, many city
and country clubs, once on the downgrade and in nearly hope-
less financial trouble, have enjoyed a startling revival as weekend sociables have taken them over. Mark Twain used to refer
to New York City's venerable Lotos Club as "my secret spot on
life's riverbank." That is what city clubs were like. They were
one-sex clubs, mostly for men, and were often characterized by
a brooding melancholy. Club life consisted in sitting in leather

armchairs and smoking pipes. But the people-liking people want a more high-powdered kind of fun and a lot more coed socializing. After persisting for some seventy years in its misogynist viewpoint, the Lotos after the war ceased to be a "quiet shaded pool" where men found shelter from the world. Today on weekends you can hear high heels clattering along its hallways and soprano laughter in the ballroom.

Only the oldest members seem to mind. "The damned women even spell it 'Lotus,' " grumped one old gentleman. But as far as the younger male members are concerned, the ladies can spell it any way they like, as long as they come to the parties.

The same has happened to country clubs out in the suburbs and exurbs. Clubs once devoted to golf have changed into family-type weekend centers that bustle with co-ed sociable pursuits like dancing, cocktailing, bridge and lessons in Japanese paperfolding. A suburban tennis club near Los Angeles once held a running two-year debate about whether to buy an adjacent acre and build a swimming pool and wading pool. Some of the older members feared such a step would harm the traditional atmosphere of the club, which was that of serious tennis. Younger members wanted to build the pool for just that reason. Finally the pool was built. Overnight the character of the club began to change.

Parents could now park their kids with the high-school girl who was hired to supervise the wading pool on weekends and could go about their tennis, drinking and socializing unhampered. This increased the demand for socializing space, so a new large bar room and drinking patio were built. These facilities attracted a host of new people-liking people into the club. They in turn began pressing for more child-parking facilities and more sociable events like costume balls and buffet suppers. The final turn of the screw, as the old members saw it, came one Saturday night when a large outdoor party spilled over onto the tennis courts. Gay likeables in hard-heeled shoes turned the level clay into a cratered moonscape. Next morning an early-arriving club employee found one of the elderly tennis players contemplating the ruins with a despondent fish-eyed stare. "This club is dead!" he announced, as though suddenly discovering a fact that should have been apparent to him long before. "It may be making a lot of money but it's dead, you hear? Dead!"

The weekender pursues companionship with a furious energy that sometimes looks a little like panic. He collects friends as one might collect stamps. He knows it would be pleasant to have a small gang of really close friends (and he sometimes thinks wistfully of his school days when he did), but what he wants today is a big, gay crowd of likeables. He emphasizes quantity more than quality. Subconsciously perhaps he feels there is safety in numbers. The more friends he has, the smaller is the likelihood that a Saturday night will find him not "doing anything." One of his worst nightmares is that of being alone while others socialize.

Friendship is one of the best defenses against loneliness. Plato gave his name to the kind of love represented by friendship in its ultimate sense. But the weekender typically distrusts his ability to find it. He is prey to a modern, specifically metropolitan, kind of loneliness. Lacking friendship, or lacking the secure feeling that he can find enough of it, he has turned to sociability as a substitute.

Look again at those revealing folk tales of our time, the advertisements. See how this product or that seeks to identify itself with likeability and the likeables. Here is a brand of cigarettes. The people smoking it are shown hanging festive decorations in what may be presumed to be a church house. Here is a soft drink, concocted we are told "for those who think young." The young-thinking sociables are dancing in somebody's family room, all liking each other vigorously. Here is a Cadillac. You will remember that General Motors has long urged this car upon us as a symbol of wealth, power and prestige. Now a subtle new ingredient has been added. "The first time you drive up in a Cadillac . . ." begins the ad. The owner and his wife or lady friend are shown arriving in evening dress for a ball or some other high-level popularity exchange. The Cadillac has somehow increased their capacity to be liked.

Here in the newspaper a certain genus of women's wear is referred to as a cocktail dress. It is a dress in which to drink cocktails, presumably. This doesn't mean it is a dress designed to resist staining by liquor or one engineered to hold the wearer upright should her own skeletal supports fail. In our ears to-day the word "cocktail" refers not only to a drink but to sociability. The advertiser's hope is that the dress will become tangled with his audience's need to be surrounded by affection-ate people.

Thus cleverly have the admen tuned in on the weekender. He spends many a Saturday afternoon hanging decorations, not because he enjoys blowing up balloons but because the decora-tion hanging is a preparty party. He enjoys driving up to social gatherings in his car. As he climbs from the car and walks to the hospitable door, he thinks happily, "I am here because other people asked me to be. Everybody knows I like people and people like me." Once inside he may lose this comfortable feeling. He may feel ignored. He may chance to find out about another party next weekend to which he hasn't been invited. It may be one of those nights in which he feels tongue-tied and unable to sparkle. He may leave the party silent and discouraged, lacking the reassurance of likeability he came seeking. Possibly this is why the Cadillac ads show the hero and heroine arriving, not leaving.

Clever fellows, those admen. But wait. Here is a curious thing. Here is a minor rash of ads, mainly for mentholated cigarettes, showing people alone. An attractive young woman is sitting in a lonesome meadow. Two thirtyish adults (the lady is barefoot) are sauntering along a brook. They are surrounded by the peace of nature, these people, not the clamor of socia-bility. What is wrong? Don't they like people, don't people

like them? Have the cigarette makers erred in judgment, con-
cocting lonesome instead of sociable flavors?

No error has been made. The authors of these ads have
seen a fact of great importance. Amid his self-imposed marathon
of sociability the weekender has cravings, sometimes, for solitude. He senses in himself a need for the tranquility that solitude can bestow. He feels solitude could soothe the bruises
his soul sustains in the trample of workday life. If only he
could get away from people for a while, he thinks, the degree
of refreshment might be enormous. As a metropolitan he has
small hope of being alone for any extended period during the
workweek, so he thinks of weekends as the time when solitude
might be found.

But he seldom finds it. It may come to him in accidental
short snatches—on a Saturday afternoon behind a lawnmower,
perhaps, or in a twilight hush before a bridge game. At such
times as these he wishes he could have more. But his problem
is like that of the hapless Tantalus, who eternally reached for
water which eternally shrank from his parched lips. The
moment the weekender thinks he may have solitude in his
grasp, it turns to loneliness.

Solitude means being by yourself and liking it. Loneliness
means not liking it. The weekender typically thinks he is
going to like it. He looks with sympathy and envy at the barefoot lady smoking the mentholated cigarette. O solitude, he
thinks, O tranquility. He promises himself he will carve an
hour or two out of a busy weekend soon to savor this rare
experience. Not this month, though. Too many things going on.
Next month, when things settle down. The weekender clings to
a childlike faith that things will settle down next month.

Eventually an opportunity for solitude comes along. He
finds a solitary woodland or a park and tries to walk there in
a ruminative manner. Perhaps a husband and wife try it
together. But all they achieve is a state of restlessness and
boredom. They may smoke mint-flavored cigarettes and even

take off their shoes. This only makes their feet hurt. Solitude still hovers beyond their reach.

These are people who have had sociability trained into their very bone. Their lives have meaning largely in terms of their relationships with other people. There can't be much meaning when there are no other people to relate with. (Husband and wife don't generally think of each other as "other people" in this sense.) Moreover they are nervous about loneliness. They don't like to be alone because they are afraid they will be lonely. And they are aware that solitary walking doesn't provide visible fun. They hope they won't happen upon a group of likeables having a picnic. They fear their aloneness will look psychopathic or will seem to have resulted from unpopularity.

Of course there are weekenders who resist the prevailing mood and are happy alone. Yet the solitary weekend pursuits are rapidly fading in proportion to the sociable pursuits. Since the end of the Second World War, there has been an almost incredible boom in sociable fun. Bowling, for instance. There were about 250,000 ten-pin bowling teams in this country in 1947 and 855,000 in 1959. Americans spent $281 million on clubs and fraternal organizations in 1945 and $744 million in 1959. The Outboard Boating Club of America guesses there were about 2½ million recreational boats in use in 1947 and 8 million in 1960.

These are massive increases, all of them near or better than threefold. Compare them with the virtual standstill of hunting, for example, a generally solitary sport. Some 12 million hunting licenses were issued in this country in 1947. In 1959 about 15 million were issued. This is a rate of growth slower than that of the country's population. Or take fishing. In view of the threefold growth in boat use you might guess that a lot more fishing is being done today than fifteen years ago. Not so. Some 13 million fishing licenses were issued in 1947 and 20 million in 1959. This rate of increase is about one-fifth that of boats on the water. Obviously people are buying boats for uses other than the quiet, contemplative sport of which Izaak Walton sang.

Sociability is important to all classes of weekenders, but particularly to those toward the top of the income and status levels. Dr. Alfred Clarke demonstrated this in his 1956 study of leisure time and job prestige. In the lowest prestige level (semiskilled and unskilled workers) he found 30.3 per cent devoting most of their weekend time to solitary craftsmanlike activities. This included home "fix-it" chores in which aloneness might have been enforced rather than chosen, but it also included craft hobbies. That percentage wasn't big, but it was bigger than among the higher prestige groups. In the next two levels (from general white-collar workers up to executives) only 21 per cent spent most of their weekend time as lone craftsmen. In the top level (professional people) the proportion was 19.9 per cent.

There are other intriguing facts on this subject in magazine audience surveys. Take a determinedly upper-crust publicaton such as *Vogue*. *Vogue* says 72 per cent of its reader families (as against roughly 20 per cent in the nation as a whole) have incomes of $7,500 a year or more, and 22 per cent are in the $25,000-and-up range. Most of the readers' husbands are in Dr. Clarke's top two levels of job prestige. What kind of social life do these families have?

A graciously frantic one. Almost nine out of every ten *Vogue* families belong to at least one club, 57 per cent belong to at least three clubs and 27 per cent belong to five clubs or more. As you might expect, these families do a lot of entertaining. They favor buffet dinners, large outdoor dinners and other big-scale social feedings (63 per cent of them entertain this way), smaller and more intimate dinner parties (50 per cent), cocktail parties (46 per cent) and card parties (34 per cent).

These are highly sociable people. Some of them don't even

like to watch television alone. Thirteen per cent favor an odd new form of likeability exchange called the TV party. A TV party is one in which, after or with drinks or a meal, the guests sit in sociable silence and watch the round-cornered screen. They may simply sit until their eyes glaze over, then shamble home to bed. Or they may watch a program of special interest, and the host's plan may be to follow it with a critique. But the critique often meanders off into ordinary social discourse. In any case the attraction of the TV party is that it offers a chance to watch the picture tube without feeling lonely, left out or unsociable. A further attraction for some is that it offers sociability while at the same time giving relief from the strain of continual conversation.

The trouble with sociability is that it sours when pursued too hard, in much the same way as fun. Close friends trust each other and don't need to worry about slights and noninvitations to parties. Casual socializers don't need to worry either, for after all what does it matter? But the weekend likeables don't take these matters casually. Being with people, inviting and being invited, shunning aloneness and its appearance—all these things are too important. The likeables worry about not being able to show up here and not making a good impression there. They scheme to get into this fun clique or gain favor with that family of high sociables. They are racked with tension. Preparing for a dinner party, the hostess may fret for days. By the time she opens the door to greet her first arriving guests, she is close to collapse and has a headache that threatens to blow off the top of her skull.

As far as anybody knows, human beings have always tended to be gregarious and have avoided loneliness. Solitary confinement has been in use as a punishment through all the history of man's nastiness to man. But the sharp, nagging, ever-present fear of being alone that we know today, the fear that reaches its utmost poignancy on weekends, is apparently a relatively

new phenomenon. It seems to be a byproduct of industrializa-
tion and exists most strongly in America, though other nations
such as Britain and Japan are now not far behind. Scanty psychiatric reports from the Soviet Union indicate many Russians
are haunted in the same way. No record exists of anything
quite like it in any earlier age.

One of its causes is undoubtedly mobility. Americans typically don't stay put long, and this is particularly true of
metropolitans. The Census Bureau's figures indicate that one
family in every five moves to a different home each year, seeking economic or social gains. Some communities and some
groups of people have an even higher move rate than that.
There are big corporations in which employees making $7,500
or more a year count on being transferred on an average of
once every three or even two years. I once knew an engineer
who had been moved ten times in eleven years.

The result is that we come and go in each other's lives.
Individuals and families meet, socialize for a few years and
part. There seems to be little chance to put down what are
called "roots," to form a close personal identification with a
town or a group of people. Dr. Richard Gordon, a psychiatrist
practising in suburban New Jersey, has made a study of mobility's effects on people. The much-moved man and woman, he
says, may be disinclined or even unable to form any but superficial relationships with others. They've been hurt by partings
in the past. They know there will be more partings in the
future. They are on guard against any depth of involvement
with people because they feel it will only cause pain in the end.
This kind of hard shell around the heart and soul may have
been built in childhood when the youngster's parents kept
moving him from town to town.

Simple lack of time also prevents deep involvement. A family moves into a town or a youngster into a school. Likeability
cliques are already formed. Penetration takes time. Then as
the newcomer begins meeting people there is a period of

mutual assessment. These are people who have come from all
over the country and all kinds of backgrounds. They must feel
each other out, sense each other's attitudes. Finally the newcomer gains full membership. But by this time some of the
people he so painstakingly befriended are moving away. In a
few years the former newcomer finds himself an oldtimer, and
eventually he too moves away.

Mobility isn't the only cause of loneliness, and it certainly
isn't the saddest. Here is the saddest: Work for its own grey
purposes has taken over friendliness and changed it into a
blank-eyed smiling mask.

David Riesman in *The Lonely Crowd* and C. Wright Mills in *White Collar* both saw this depressing phenomenon gaining ascendancy in the peacetime boom economy after World War II. Machines were fast replacing people in the actual production (Mills liked to use the word "manipulation") of *things*. People in the workday world were therefore more and more concerned with the manipulation of symbols representing the things and with the manipulation of other people. These workers made up the growing army of white-collar folk about whom Mills was so worried. To do their jobs successfully—indeed to get their jobs in the first place—they had to have winning personalities. They had to sell themselves. Every day they smiled for pay.

Some jobs require more personal charm than others, of course. The pretty receptionist, the honey-voiced girl who answers the phone, the dynamic executive, the warm-hearted fellow on TV who warns us about the vile chemicals that seethe through our internal pipes: these are obvious examples of what Mills called the "marketing personality." But even engineers, accountants and typists who may seldom make contacts outside the company find it necessary to weave a false personal fabric around the job. In a world where people lack physical things to show for a day's work, and where job competence is at least partly a matter of subjective judgment, personal charm is felt to be a key to success.

Inevitably this prostitution of human warmth must sour the contacts people make over the weekend. "We cannot so easily separate coercive friendliness on the job from a spontaneous expression of genuine friendliness off the job," Riesman wrote. Friendliness is cheapened because all week we feel it being used to influence us. A smile on a child's face is a lovely thing. On an adult's face it may be trash. The smiler may simply be trying to sell us a deodorant.

"The cash nexus that links one man to another in transient contact has been made subtle in a dozen ways and made to bite deeper into all areas of life and relations," Mills wrote bit-

terly. "People are required by the salesman ethic and con-
vention to pretend interest in others in order to manipulate
them. In the course of time, as this ethic spreads, it is got on
to." Everybody knows what is going on, everybody has the
feeling of being constantly and secretly manipulated. "Men are
estranged from one another as each secretly tries to make an
instrument of the other."

Underlying the weekender's relationships is the corrosive
suspicion of veiled purposes, devious designs. Why is he butter-
ing me up, the weekender wonders when somebody is nice to
him. What does he want? Information? A job? To be invited
to my party? To borrow my half-inch drill? The pleasant
thought may drift into the weekender's mind that the show
of affection which so puzzles him may actually have no hidden
purpose. But he can seldom quite believe it.

Actually writers like Sinclair Lewis and F. Scott Fitzgerald
noted all this back in the 1920's. George Babbitt was a typical
marketing personality and desperately lonely. Jay Gatsby gave
lavish parties attended by hundreds of sociables, but only a
handful of mourners turned up at his funeral. Yet from a
statistical point of view this was only half as important in 1920
as it is now. Back then, only 25 per cent of gainfully employed
Americans were in white-collar jobs. In 1961 the proportion was
48 per cent and still climbing toward nobody knows what limit.

Thus the weekender often finds it hard to feel close to
people. His attempts at contact are frustrated further by the
weekend requirement that one be gay. He sees only the smiling
surface of his fellow likeables. A housewife who lives in the
home neighborhood all week has perhaps a better chance than
her husband to see behind her friends' weekend masks. The
husband may feel closer to the people he knows at work. He
feels he has more in common with them. They have meaning to
him in terms of his earnings. His weekend friends may be only
that—weekend friends, people by whom to be liked until Sunday night, then forgotten.

"I have a headache every Saturday night, and I know why,"

a housewife told Detroit psychiatrist Jean Rosenbaum. "It's because I have to smile all the time. If I could let my face relax I wouldn't get headaches."

Compulsive weekend socializing today begins in early grade school. A child who spends large expanses of weekend time alone is felt to be maladjusted. His parents worry about him. His emotional sensing equipment isn't yet finely tuned enough to tell him extended solitude is thought unhealthy and improper.

But he will learn soon enough. He will soon find himself in dancing class, the church children's club and other organizations which his parents deem useful in teaching likeability. His mother will canvass the town for suitable playmates, and he will visit or be visited each weekend. He will be a guest and occasional host at Saturday afternoon birthday parties, from which he will reel home bloated and racked with hiccups. After each such party the exhausted hostess-mother will survey the wreckage of her living room and swear never to do this to herself again. But she swore similar oaths in years past. It is altogether likely that her own war with loneliness will continue to keep her child's weekends teeming with people as are her own.

Compulsive people-liking is motivated by a youngster's parents at first, but as he progresses through school the motivation comes increasingly from within himself. Indeed much of its basis may be laid down in the very classrooms which he leaves so joyously each Friday afternoon. In grade schools today teachers concentrate heavily on making the small weekender a social success. I remember once listening in dismay while a kindergarten teacher explained this philosophy. The single thing she hoped to accomplish was "group adjustment." All childish attempts at solitude were to be squashed. The teacher's assumption was that the lone child could not be happy. She was expressing her own, the school's and the taxpayers' fear of loneliness.

By the time a boy or girl reaches college, the need to be sociable on weekends is usually well entrenched. The young adult now doesn't believe it is either pleasant or smart to be alone. He typically equates high sociability with sophistication. He has perceived that any drab personality can be surrounded by other people on workdays, for this is the nature of education and work in the metropolitan society. On weekends the individual is at liberty to be by himself, but to be surrounded by others requires sociable skills and is therefore a basis on which to claim prestige.

Popularity becomes the college student's credo. He works hard to polish the smiling aspects of his personality. Sex plays a big role in his world of course. Courting as we know it involves socializing. The college student is aware that before he is likely to enjoy sexual experience, he must learn skills such as ballroom dancing, small talk and restaurant French. But sex isn't normally the single object of his efforts to be likeable. He doesn't go to a party simply for the petting he hopes will take place afterward. He goes to be with people and prove to himself again that he is attractive to them. If sex were his single object, he would want to go somewhere alone with his date.

That is the last thing he wants. Indeed, at big men's campuses like Princeton and Yale, where girls are invited for football and dance weekends, the young male weekenders go to extreme lengths to escape the terror of finding themselves alone with their dates. Starting a week or two before the big event, they restlessly roam the campus, wangling invitations to parties and lining up group activities. The happiest young fellow on Friday night is the one who can show his friends a two-day schedule so tightly packed with sociable activity that not a chill minute of blank time remains.

The college social failure is among the saddest figures of our time. The grind, as we used to call him, could at one time manage to carve out a reasonably happy life for himself. He wasn't popular, but this didn't bother him very much in a society that didn't attach such desperate importance to sociability. The serious young scholar could find companionship among other serious scholars, of whom there was no shortage. He could bask in the professors' admiration and sometimes in their friendship. He could spend Saturdays in the library without feeling ashamed.

Today both the grind and his opposite, the high-timing College Joe, are growing scarce on campus. The aim of today's college students is to be good organization men. They want to be graciously well-rounded. Typically they look forward to lives as big-company employees or big-company wives. They know they must pay attention in the lecture hall. And since most of them have come up through group-adjustment schools, they also know they must learn social skills. Even the professors, who today often earn income as corporate consultants and lecturers, may feel the likeability training of the campus is almost as important as what is learned in class. It isn't unusual for a professor to call in some favored scholarly student and urge him to participate more in campus weekend life. In the days before World War II this would have been a startling turn of events.

Thus the student who doesn't feel like socializing is in a barely tenable position. All around him is the feeling that he is not only odd but foolish. Even unhappier is the student who wants to be sociable but can't. Perhaps he or she is shy or not fair of face. The people-liking people won't let him like them. He feels cut off from the mainstream of life. On weekends he is likely to shun the campus. Or he may go to the movies with a few friends in like straits. But theirs is a reluctant company. Each yearns to move into the more brilliant social planes above.

After college the weekender may find his socializing compulsion relaxed for a time. Often the young white-collar man or woman takes an apartment in a city. To the newly arrived, a city appears to have no definite society and to make no social demands. You can live there for years without ever meeting your neighbors. The bachelor or bachelor girl may feel unhappy about weekends spent alone but at least isn't deviled by the shame of revealing this aloneness to a known social group. Moreover as he roams the city streets or eats a stale sandwich in a cafeteria he sees other lone individuals around him. The city is where loners gravitate.

Of course in time he may find a group of single sociables in the city. Or he may travel on weekends to some place where they gather: a ski lodge, a lake, a boat club or his old home town. Some suburban towns have a regular Friday-night immigration of former high-school gangs. But the single weekender's need to be likeable isn't nearly so pressing as it was in college or as it will probably be later in his life. Bathed in the city's vast indifference, he is at liberty to spend an occasional contented weekend alone. E. B. White once said of New York City that it bestows the "jewel of solitude." It bestows even more than that: the jewel of choice.

Eventually our bachelor or bachelor girl gets married. Typically the new young family moves to the city's outskirts or to the suburbs, into a weedily gracious garden apartment or a low-cost housing development. Here sociability is required.

In such a neighborhood the women are likely to be lonely at first, particularly those who had careers before marriage. With the children's help they get to know each other. The husbands, home on weekends, meet the neighbors their wives have befriended. Soon one family invites a few others to drop in for a drink. Other families, noting this, feel left out. No night is more lonesome than a Saturday night in a thin-walled apartment, with a loud party in progress next door or across the courtyard—a party that includes people you know. To avoid suffering through more such nights, the families now begin to cultivate each other's weekend friendship.

Early in the 1950's William H. Whyte, Jr., who later went on to write *The Organization Man*, studied a young-married community called Park Forest, near Chicago. Park Forest is a vast housing development with dwelling units arranged around courtyards. At the time Whyte surveyed this typical scene, many of the residents were young college graduates starting the long climb in mighty corporations. Most planned to move in a few years to larger homes. But the transient nature of their occupancy at Park Forest didn't deter them from collecting weekend friends greedily. Their weekends were spent determinedly liking other people, even those they didn't like. They were in church and school groups, civic committees, children's service outfits, sport clubs and hobby clubs. And of course they were in Saturday night social cliques.

"Outgoing" was a word of highest praise in this community of young likeables, Whyte wrote in *Fortune*. "Not in solitary and selfish contemplation but in doing things with other people does one fulfill oneself. . . . There is a tendency to equate the lone individual with psychic disorder."

Whyte noted that many of these were people who in later years (which is to say, just about now) would emerge as business leaders and weekend social leaders in their middle- and upper-middle-class circles. They were people who valued group harmony more than privacy. (They left their doors unlocked as a symbol of friendliness.) Group harmony to them meant more than a passive absence of friction. It meant actively seeking out one's neighbors, actively reaffirming the group's solidarity at every opportunity.

The Park Foresters seemed moderately happy to Whyte and his fellow researchers. But Whyte wondered how "good" the happiness was. How much was real, how much was just the mask of likeability? The more determinedly cohesive the group, he pointed out, the rougher life is on the ostracized. And as he also pointed out: "Many sense that by immersing themselves in the group, they are frustrating their other urges." Among the sociables it is hard to enjoy a solitary walk or a Saturday evening with your phonograph. If you want to listen to Mozart or watch TV, you've got to have other people in to help you.

In time the successful Park Forest family graduates to a more costly apartment in the city or a house in Shaker Heights, Wilmette or Grosse Pointe. The fear of being left out travels with the family furniture in the moving van. In the wealthier suburbs the houses are widely spaced and doors are locked. This bestows an only half-wanted weekend privacy on the residents. Many miss the college-dorm-like atmosphere of the neighborhoods they knew as young marrieds, where friends dropped in without knocking. But privacy is a privilege of the wealthy and for status purposes must be visibly used. Somewhat reluctantly the homeowner spends a weekend or two building a fence around his property. But it is a rather strange kind of fence. It is more a boundary marker than a barrier. It is likely to be a split rail or some similar design, over which, through which or under which children can climb. It proclaims the delicate state of sociable privacy. It says, "This place is as private as anything, but everybody is welcome."

The art of liking people now is worked on a wider canvas than among the young marrieds. The weekender is among higher-salaried people with bigger houses and apartments. Parties tend to be bigger in proportion. The weekender must hunt hard to find enough weekend friends to fill his new living room. He may have small intimate dinner and card parties, but once in a while he feels the need for a full assembly at which he can show how many weekend friends he really has. At these large likeability exchanges he hopes to count at least one man or woman for every four square feet of living room. The high sociables have more, of course. Their friends overflow throughout the house or apartment.

Thus the rising weekender must look far to fill out his collection. If he is a suburbanite, he must look well beyond his immediate neighborhood. A subtle new requirement compels him to do this in any case. Among the more accomplished suburban likeables there is a feeling that any drab family can make weekend friends of the people who happen to live next door. As the college student saw that it takes no skill to have companions on workdays, they see that it takes none to live in a chummy neighborhood. If you really want to show your likeability, you should have friends all over town.

This requires work and patience. Man and wife together must join groups such as the PTA or the church social club— or, if they can afford it, the country club. Once they are in, their fine-tuned sensing equipment (Riesman called it "radar") quickly tells them which couples are the fun leaders or the most highly sociable. They aim their smiles toward these people.

The high sociables are at the top of the weekend status pyramid. The pyramid isn't designed according to wealth and social origin alone but also according to fun capacity and like-ability. These rankings sometimes coincide but not always. To be a weekend fun or social leader you need enough wealth to afford fun equipment, liquor, babysitters, a house or apartment suitable for entertaining and other requirements. But the mere having of wealth isn't enough to make you a leader of weekend society. Similarly you need the kind of social background that has trained you to like people efficiently. But "breeding" in the old sense is not by itself a strong enough magnet to attract large numbers of likeables around you. In the weekend society the things that count most are the abilities to have and cause fun and to be an opiate for loneliness.

A survey of this phenomenon was conducted in 1962 in a medium-sized Connecticut suburb. The survey drew forth the names of seven families that were almost universally considered to be high sociables. Among these families, one was unquestion-ably wealthy. Two more were somewhat wealthier than the town norm. Three were ordinary middle-class families. And one was in the town's lower income bracket.

High sociables are usually surrounded by a close clique of people who are always together on weekends and like each other with nervous ferocity. Some may even be real friends. This inner group is surrounded in turn by a large outer group of people who sometimes get invited to the high sociables' parties and picnics. Those on the outer rim like the inner-rim people frantically but receive fewer smiles back from the hub than they feed in. The newcomer couple seeking membership must usually begin with a probationary period on the outer rim, and with luck may edge toward the center in time.

But if denied membership the newcomers will have to seek a way into some less brilliant, smaller group—perhaps a group of weekenders who are operating without fun leaders. Such groups drift dimly out beyond the outer rims of major likeability circles. They are often rather forlorn. Some of course are composed of close friends and are not much interested in the sociable scramble. But in others the bond of weekend friendship may be strained by the same reluctance that marks the college students who go to movies on Saturday night. They like each other dutifully but not very energetically.

Amid this kind of pressure, ever desperately hunting smiles, the weekender may live most of the Saturdays and Sundays in his adult life. But when his children are grown, he may move back to the city whose magnetism few metropolitans can ever fully escape. Or he may have bucked the tide in the first place and made his home in the city. Here the need to be sociable is not commonly as great as in the suburbs. But the city dweller is haunted by loneliness too. He may not be reminded of it as many times a weekend as the suburbanite, but it is often with him, a dark shadow following him through crowded streets.

Typically the city dweller lives among neighbors whom he knows only well enough to warrant an occasional "good morning." It's true there are some apartment houses where the atmosphere of a college dorm prevails, and room-to-room parties thunder on weekends. But this is the exception. A Brooklyn College sociologist, Sylvia Fleis Fava, once compared the amount of "neighboring" that went on in mid-city Manhattan and suburban Long Island. In Manhattan, she found, 36 per cent of the residents pay little or no attention to their neighbors, while in the suburban community only 10 per cent fall in this aloof category. The city family is more likely to draw its weekend friends from the husband's and wife's present and earlier careers.

It is a rare city family that gets into half as many civic,

church or children's service organizations as the suburban weekender. As far back as the early 1940's Mayor LaGuardia of New
York was grumbling that his city was suffering from a shortage
of volunteer civic spirit. The spirit was being siphoned off into
the suburbs. One reason was New York's shortage of housing
attractive to middle-income people, who are the backbone of
civic life in most towns. But another important reason was that
New Yorkers in general, like city people almost everywhere,
don't feel a pressing need on weekends to go out and make
themselves known around town.

What city dwellers do like to do on weekends is to be invited
out of the city. They like to be house guests of friends who own
cottages on lakes and at the sea shore, houses on the rural fringe
or even ordinary homes in the suburbs. Perhaps they feel country or suburban life offers more opportunities for the outdoor
type of visible fun. Perhaps they like the ease with which they
can pick up fun badges like sunburn, mosquito bites and
skinned knuckles. Some of them like the high-voltage sociability
of country-club life. All this gives them material with which to
brag to city likeables next weekend. At any rate their weekend
sociability is often centrifugal, drawing them from the city in
hordes that clog the highways Friday night.

Some good-hearted suburbanites, exurbanites and shore-
cottage owners play host to the city centrifugals twice or more
a month all through spring and summer. "If they like it here
so much, why don't they *move* here?" cried an overworked
housewife on the metropolitan fringe one Sunday night, survey-
ing the vast piles of dirty dishes that littered her kitchen. The
answer was confided to a friend the very next weekend by one
of her more regular guests. "It's nice out here," he said, "but
the commute would kill me."

The country dwellers or suburbanites are usually anxious to
prove to the centrifugals that it is foolish to live in a crowded,
noisy city. "We love it out here," the host tells his city friend
as they stroll outdoors after Saturday lunch. "There's room to
move around, you know?" The guest, who is having trouble

hearing above the howl of a neighbor's power mower, utters some polite noises. He kicks to shake out something that is crawling up the inside of his trouser leg. A cynical counter-gambit occurs to him. "Say," he says casually, "I wonder if you'd show me where to get some cigarettes. Is it far?" Of course it is far. In fact the nearest store is the equivalent of perhaps thirty city blocks distant. But the host rises to the challenge instantly. "Sure," he says. "It'll give me a chance to show you the town. Quaint little place. Peaceful . . ." And thus do the two breeds of metropolitan needle each other through the weekend.

On Saturday afternoon there may be a swim or a boat ride, during which the host discourses proudly on the advantage of living so close to water and the guest asks whether there are always this many large, hairy, carnivorous flies at the beach. On Saturday night there may be a dance at the club or a large noisy party held outdoors beneath the moon, which nobody can see because there is a thick overcast. The moon never shines when fringe dwellers are trying to prove a point to city dwellers.

But the house guest is likely to enjoy the likeability exchange. He is a natural alien and as such may become an ear for confessions, confidences and complaints which the local sociables have been longing to get off their chests. This may please him, though he is likely to keep the fact secret. He now considers himself an honorary member of a social clique which, he likes to think, is probably hard for most people to get into.

By Sunday noon the guests and their hosts are all wishing the visit had been shorter. All are drained with fatigue and yearning to lie down and go to sleep. In the long silences that fall among them, it is possible to hear the rhythmic thump of headaches pulsating within skulls. Predinner drinks may perk everybody up somewhat, but fatigue's leaden weight settles down again by dessert time. The strain of being gay for two straight days is becoming almost unbearable. The once-likeable smiles now have a frantic and rather pop-eyed look. A lady

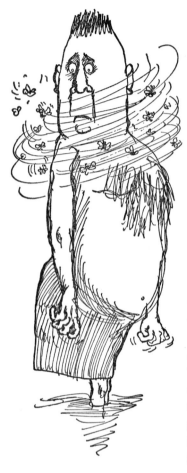

guest may begin a feeble protest that she will help with the dishes. The hostess insists she will do them later. The guest hastily agrees. Finally, to everyone's enormous relief, the guests take their leave. Everybody realizes something that all will have forgotten by next weekend. Too much sociability, too tightly compressed, with too few reviving periods of solitude interspersed, is as bad as no sociability at all.

And there is something else most of the likeables may realize. Sociability can be one of the more pleasant ways of spending weekend time. People themselves are a rich source of fun for each other. But when people-liking becomes too urgent a matter, it ceases to be so pleasant. Then the weekend's promise of peace gets lost, and the weekender returns to work on Monday with a feeling of weariness and glum exasperation.

I stepped out of a dinner dance one hot Saturday night to find a cooling breeze. After a while a woman came out and stood nearby. "I wish they'd hold the dance out here in the dark," she said. "Then nobody would know whether I was smiling or not. I've been smiling for three straight hours. My whole face aches."

I agreed, unconsciously smiling at her in the darkness.

6. Feasts of Alcohol and Affection

ETHYL ALCOHOL is a remarkable substance which, when mixed with a weekender, produces sociability. Weekenders don't often drink it alone. It comes into evidence when two or more (usually more) of them get together, wishing to like each other. It is the oil in the complex emotional machinery of parties.

There are many reasons why people drink alcohol, of course. Some simply like the taste of alcoholic beverages. Some seek confidence to help them face difficult tasks. Others seek forgetfulness of painful facts, escape from personal prisons or a lift out of some valley of the blues. Weekend drinking at various times and in individual cases may have these motives behind it. But there is another motive that stands out above the others, a motive that is characteristic of weekend drinking almost everywhere and almost always. The purpose of drink on weekends is to anesthetize the tensions that exist between people and allow an easygoing comradeship.

Martha Wolfenstein, early observer of the fun mystique, noted "an increased tendency to attempt by drinking to reduce constraints sufficiently so that we can have fun." Perhaps she should have added "with each other." A weekend gathering at which liquor is served is a venture in cooperative constraint loosening.

In fact for many people this is virtually the only important motive for drinking. These people, and possibly they add up to a majority of metropolitans, do little or no drinking except on weekends when it is necessary to be gay and likeable. Of course there are many who drink almost as much or more on workdays. The liquid lunch is ordinary among the talent elite, for instance. But taverns and restaurants beyond the downtown office neighborhoods, and particularly package liquor stores, conduct their liveliest business as a rule on Fridays and Saturdays. The weekend is when most people most want to drink.

The weekend periodicity of drinking shows up in an oblique but rather startling way in some of the liquor industry's records. In the year 1960 Americans poured down about one and a third gallons of distilled spirits per capita. That is no thimbleful and should give the liquor makers no cause for alarm. But their eyes tend to blur with tears when they contemplate the drinking habits of some of our forefathers. In 1860 the annual per-capita consumption was something like three and a quarter gallons.

These statistics seem to contradict the current popular caricature of an American as a man on a treadmill, able to stand the pain only by dulling it with tranquilizers and alcohol. The figures become still more puzzling when you consider that there are fewer abstainers in the population today. In 1860 a great many people, maybe the majority and especially women, abstained totally or drank only an occasional glass of wine or beer. Today the majority are not abstainers. In particular the old social barriers against women's drinking have been all but torn down. Nonabstention is particularly notable in the generation that began adult life in the 1940's and in the new generations now following. Among adults aged up to fifty, according to a number of recent studies by sociologists, only a quarter or so never drink. Among those aged over sixty, more than half don't drink. Medical reasons are involved here, of course, but social pressures play a big part. Adults whose

traditions are rooted in the postwar age feel in general that it is neither sophisticated nor sociable to refuse strong drink.

Then why was the per-capita consumption of liquor so high a hundred years ago? Part of the answer seems to lie, oddly, in the fact that there were no weekends as we know them. People who did drink hard liquor tended to drink indiscriminately on all days of the week, and so tended to drink a lot. A far larger proportion than today performed unskilled manual labor and could drink on the job without becoming too inefficient. In fact beer and even whiskey were considered a normal part of a man's wages in some work groups. In our vastly more complicated society on-the-job drinking can't be so casually tolerated in most occupations. Industrial workers whose jobs take them near dangerous machines must be forbidden to drink for their own and others' safety. Those performing delicate handwork must also shun alcohol during the workday. And despite the example set by the three-Gibson lunches of the talent elite, the general feeling among white-collar people and their employers is that drink decreases the efficiency of those who must work with their brains. Housewives at home, meanwhile, though they can drink on weekends with a clear conscience, still face a social taboo against drinking at home on a workday.

Even when the day's work is ended, the evening is still overshadowed by work and its constraints. Since we must be up bright-eyed and early tomorrow, we can't afford to carouse tonight. Some toss down a drink or two on work nights, but most control their intake quite strictly, knowing the weekend is coming with its promise of release. The workers of 1860 were not dominated by so powerful a seven-day rhythm and when a man wanted a drink, he drank. Though his consumption on any single day might be moderate, his week's total was likely to be greater than that of the typical weekender.

The inexorable rhythm even dominates alcoholics in their early stages. The alcoholic often begins his slide to doom by becoming drunk on weekends. Dr. E. M. Jellinek of Yale University, well-known student of alcoholism, reported in the *Quarterly Journal of Studies on Alcohol* that heavy weekend drinking typically precedes weekday drunkenness in the disease's normal course. Among men Dr. Jellinek studied, the first weekend drunkenness occurred at the average age of 27.2

years. Midweek drunkenness started at 30.4 years. The weekend is the time when getting high is allowed and even encouraged, and outright drunkenness is regarded with amused tolerance. During the workweek the developing alcoholic feels greater constraints against drinking.

In this he doesn't differ from the ordinary weekender, except in degree. The weekend is the time for letting loose, and ethyl alcohol is the great loosener. It loosens the inhibitions and the tongue (and sometimes, so it seems, the bony plates of the skull). It helps the weekenders feast joyfully on each other's affections.

Ethyl alcohol began playing a part in man's history long before anybody began recording the history. Nobody knows where or in what shining hour the first drinker tasted a fermented liquid and felt the winds of eternity blowing through his brain. But the discovery was enthusiastically welcomed. As Berton Roueché notes in *The Neutral Spirit,* no record exists of any agricultural society in which alcoholic drink was unknown. Indeed there were probably some societies in which grain was raised to make beer before anybody ever thought of making bread. Man as far back as we can see him has felt a need for what Roueché calls "release from the intolerable clutch of reality."

In this respect the weekenders are probably not much different from the mead drinkers of millennia ago. But they differ in the kind of reality from which they seek release. And they differ in the rituals by which they approach the release. The weekenders drink under all kinds of circumstances and in all kinds of places: in taverns and restaurants, at clubs, at football games and Little League games, in boats and on skis. But the place where they drink most often and most typically is the living room.

They may be gathered for an afternoon cocktail party, a dinner, a card game or a nighttime party. The gathering takes

place in an ordinary home (sometimes on a patio or in a backyard), and it is attended by both men and women.

Coed home drinking parties have been fashionable for a
long time among the very rich, those with grand ballrooms and
servants to fix the drinks. But among middle-class Americans
in general, the two-sex home alcohol feast has become popular
only in recent times. Its development into what we know today
is the weekenders' own special contribution to the ages-old art
of drinking.

Its short history has not always been honorable. It rose to
popularity during the Prohibition era. Before that time most
drinking in America was done by men in taverns and clubs.
Prohibition forced the development of speakeasies, which were
glamorously naughty and in later years made a fine background
for television gangster shows. But probably more important
sociologically was the fact that drinking was driven into the
home.

Prohibition happened to coincide with women's suffrage and
a general stiffening of feminine backbone. Not all women were
content to sit knitting in an upstairs bedroom while the men,
driven home from their taverns, caroused below. The women
demanded to be let in on the fun. Thus the home drinking
party became established as a coed affair.

When Prohibition was repealed, a good many men went
back to their male drinking retreats. But many had found they
liked drinking coeducationally. So had many women. Liquor,
sex and the general weekend reaching-out for affection mixed
pleasingly to produce some subtle new flavors. The home alcohol feast thus remained a fact of weekend life. It grew more
and more prominent as the fun mystique and the people-liking
compulsion grew stronger. In the days before Prohibition probably not more than 25 per cent of liquor was imbibed at home.
The bulk of it was sold by the drink at taverns, restaurants
and other establishments. By 1940, according to *Spirits* Magazine, 49 per cent of the distilled spirits sold in this country

was carried home in the bottle. And by 1960 the proportion had reached 71 per cent.

There are alcohol feasts on workdays too of course. Some are sociable in nature. Many are conducted for business purposes and are simply extensions of the marketplace of smiles. Executives take each other home for dinner. Corporations throw cocktail parties in connection with new-product unveilings and other announcements about which, in the absence of free booze, nobody might give a hoot. None of this has much in common with the typical weekend gathering. On Saturday the weekender needs to find out how much people will smile at him when they don't want him to buy, agree to, be interested in or do anything. Some weekend parties have underlying business purposes, but most represent sociability in its pure form.

One of the few systematic studies of drinking parties was conducted in the late 1950's by a group at the University of Chicago: David Riesman, Robert J. Potter and Jeanne Watson. Together and separately they attended 80 parties in and around Chicago for what they called "participant observation." Upon recovering they reported their findings in *Human Organization* and in *Psychiatry: Journal for the Study of Interpersonal Processes*. They were surprised to find how little people were aware of the roles they played at likeability exchanges or "of the phases through which parties pass, other than those which conclude by people passing out." They were struck by how little people remembered parties or enjoyed them retrospectively "as part of one's emotional subsoil."

Possibly the reason for this is that the structure and workings of weekend parties are vague, almost entirely emotional and extremely hard to translate into logical terms. As the Chicago partygoers remarked of sociability, "There are no clear standards as to what constitutes adequate performance." The weekender knows he must perform well, but he isn't sure exactly how. He knows he must like other members of the gathering and yearns to be liked in return, but the exchange of affection, if any, must be indirect and only dimly visible. It must take place beneath a shimmering surface of small talk about antique furniture or medium talk about the New Frontier. The partygoer often can't know whether he has succeeded or, if so, how well. Indeed, he often has no clear idea of what he is succeeding or failing at.

The rules are particularly vague at large cocktail parties. The guest is simply asked to come, drink and like, shotgun or wide-angle fashion. Only a little less vague is the intimate dinner-and-conversation party, where the focus of liking is smaller. The guest has somewhat clearer guidelines at the gathering in which he is told in general terms what to do—a bridge party, for instance, or one devoted to charades or dramatic readings. He knows what constitutes adequate performance in a card game. But he must still succeed in likeability. No type of party is immune to failure.

And when it fails there is no basis by which to affix blame. The blame floats diffusely through the group and enshrouds all, host and guests alike. At the large party they stand about awkwardly in tight clumps, listening to the deepening silence. Corners of the room seem to grow dark as loneliness seeps in through the cracks. The high sociables begin to leave. Perhaps, having had more experience, they know a party that has begun to wind down can't often be revived. The others cling to hope for a while and stay on. But eventually they, too, drift to the bedroom and their coats. The host and hostess dart about unhappily, trying to dam the tide that flows out of their front door. Finally their living room is empty. They stand amid the debris, blaming themselves. But each of the guests on his way through the desolate night blames himself too. Nobody ever knows whose fault it was. Nor does anybody know just what it was that went wrong. Somehow the hoped-for flood of mutual affection failed to materialize, and each member's capacity for warmth stayed locked inside him.

At the smaller dying party the guests can't leave at their own discretion but must sit cemented to their chairs, each hoping another will make the first move for the door. They converse nervously in short bursts. Each hopes somebody will do something to fan the dimming embers of sociability, but nobody knows what to do. As at the larger gathering, each blames himself.

Being at such a party is like being a character in a Franz Kafka novel. You are on trial for some crime whose nature hasn't been made clear to you. You don't know what the law is in any case. You have no way to defend yourself. You end by agreeing you're guilty, though you still don't quite know of what.

People are infinite in their variety and every party is unique. But there are general similarities among certain types of parties, and sometimes you can see them going through phases in a quite orderly way.

In terms of size weekend gatherings can be divided into three classes. There are those with twenty or more members, those with ten or fewer and those in between. In the Chicago partygoers' observation the in-between size seemed least likely to succeed. Such a gathering is too large for intimacy or a sharp focus of liking and too small for free-drifting sociability. Fifteen people in a room can't all communicate with each other at once. Yet there aren't enough of them to break into fluid subgroups among which they can circulate.

What often happens at such a party is that a random seating arrangement occurs and then becomes frozen. The partygoers find themselves in subgroups from which they can't escape. At one end of the room women discuss food shopping. Men at the other end are talking about carburetors. A group clustered about the sofa is criticizing the school system. Interspersed may be a racked few who are trying to tune in on two groups at once. There are also some whose seat positions attach them to the wrong groups. A woman sits near the men and listens gloomily to their talk of cars. She feels bolted to her chair. It takes a major upheaval, such as the hostess' announcing coffee will be served in the dining room, to effect any movement.

And if the guests are asked to carry their coffee back to the living room, they will almost invariably go back to the same positions they had before. This will be true even if the host or hostess has artfully provided fewer chairs than there are people, forcing some guests to stand and hoping thereby to create movement. It doesn't always work. At one such gathering after a forced upheaval I watched a man go back to the exact spot where he had stood before, next to a hi-fi set whose top was cluttered with china figures. He crossed his legs in exactly the same way and picked up the same figure he had been toying with before. It is as though the members of such a group become frustrated by the way channels of affection have been clogged, and each retires into some dim cell of his own. Eventually all the subgroups sink into a morose lethargy as each member realizes he is trapped for all the party's eternity. The talk grows sporadic. Tongues cleave to the roofs of mouths.

The Kafka-like trial is moving toward its squirming climax. Host and guests see they have failed and must be judged guilty. Usually there is somebody who utters the awful words. "Well," says the self-appointed judge, "we're a wide-awake bunch tonight, aren't we?" A hollow croaking laugh goes up from the doomed defendants. Within a few minutes the guests are stampeding through the door.

Drinking parties with twenty or more members are less likely to fail. But there is always the danger that they will break into subparties of the difficult in-between size, which subsequently freeze. This is particularly true of city parties, in cases where two or more rooms of an apartment are available to the members. Older marrieds may cluster in one room while young marrieds dance in another, and in a dim alcove single men make time with single girls. Suburban party personnel are more homogeneous and have less obvious a basis by which to classify themselves into subparties. Moreover a suburbanite arriving at a large popularity exchange often knows at least half the people there and doesn't feel shy about moving from group to group, particularly after his first drink or two.

City likeables typically operate in more loose-knit circles and are less likely to know everbody at each other's big gatherings. This is notably characteristic of the single. They give and attend parties as much to make new weekend contacts as to reaffirm old ones. Sometimes a bachelor or bachelor girl, or a group of roommates, will throw a party and instruct each invitee to bring one or more guests of his own. Thus the host may be to some extent a stranger at his own party.

A party such as this can be and often is crashed. Men students from Tulane University used to wander around New Orleans' French Quarter on hot Saturday nights and listen for the sounds of a party coming from an open window. Upon locating one, they'd knock on the door and say, "Cora invited us." If they were lucky the member at the door would either assume there was a Cora present or, being mellowed by alcohol, wouldn't care one way or the other, and the Tulane men would enter the sociable scene. They exemplified the typical weekender view that any kind of sociability, even among strangers, is better than a lone Saturday night. The collegiate weekender especially is likely to seek a party for its own sake, quite apart from any wish he may have to exchange affection with particular people who are there. He prefers the flushed excitement and superficial liking of strangers at a drinking party to the quieter, more real affection he might find with one or two close friends. For a brief hour at a large gathering he is able to believe a whole load of love is being heaped upon him. Of course most of it will have evaporated by the next morning.

It may be significant that weekenders don't often refer to large drinking parties as such. They seem reluctant to admit that the purpose of such a party is to drink, and to imply thereby that chemical help is necessary for the giving and receiving of love. In the middle and upper-middle classes big drinking parties are most often called cocktail parties, whether or not the beverage served is the short, hard, mixed drink which the word cocktail specifically means. It somehow seems less blunt to call it a cocktail party than a drinking party.

Laboring-class people seldom use the word cocktail because it has a snobbish ring to their ears. They have euphemisms of their own. Often when they get the urge to do some big-crowd drinking, they seek an excuse such as somebody's getting married, graduating, going away somewhere or returning from somewhere. The party gets its name from its particular excuse. It is almost always held on a weekend, usually a Saturday night, whether or not the event in question occurs on the weekend.

In the lower white-collar group large drinking parties are generally less frequent. Possibly this is because many of these people are deeply immersed in status striving and spend heavily on houses, clothes, cars and other badges of rank. They often have little cash left on weekends with which to buy the vast gallonage of liquor required by a big party. Young sociables on the way up also fall in this category. Among them small intimate parties are the general rule. If they do sometimes have a large gathering, it is likely to be a bring-your-own-bottle affair.

A big weekend popularity exchange usually begins when a host or hostess decides the time has come, begins wondering whom to invite and immediately wishes the whole thing could be forgotten. The trouble is that a large party is one to which everybody expects to be invited. Small intimate parties are obviously not for everybody. The uninvited likeable may feel a pang, but he eventually concludes he'll be invited to your next small gathering. He theorizes perhaps that you didn't think he went with this weekend's group but will fit neatly into next weekend's. Or he recognizes that he stands at an outer rim of your sociability circle and that your dinner party is for inner-rim people. He knows you must draw the line somewhere.

But with a big drinking party there is no convenient or obvious place to draw any kind of line. Somewhere on or beyond the outer rim there is bound to be somebody who considers himself invitable and, rebuffed, becomes your casual social enemy.

When the hour of the party arrives, the first guests to show up are often a European couple who believe in promptness and a few others who are going to another bash later. The party goes through a difficult phase, temporarily in the no-man's-land between ten and twenty members. The host and hostess, their nerves screwed as taut as banjo strings, seem to give off a high-pitched twang as they attempt conversation. But then other guests begin to arrive. Gradually at first, then at an accelerating pace, alcohol seeps into people. The talk grows louder. Guests begin to put their arms around each other and grasp each other's elbows, their yearning for affection now openly displayed. Some sway as trees in the wind. Everybody's clothing, so carefully donned, takes on a snowlike dusting of cigarette ash. The party is approaching its peak of sociability.

A phenomenon called "overshooting" is now taking place. The word was first used in this sense by Dr. Giorgio Lolli, former director of the Yale Plan Clinic for Alcoholics and a fascinated student of weekend drinking. The typical partygoer really needs only one or two drinks for the loosening effect he wants. But while waiting for these two to pass into his bloodstream and reach his brain, he impatiently drinks two more. Then all four wallop him at once.

This is particularly likely to happen, Dr. Lolli says, at afternoon cocktail parties and in the premeal drinking periods at dinner parties. Alcohol imbibed with or right after a square meal enters the bloodstream much more slowly than otherwise. But the Saturday afternoon or evening partygoer drinks on an empty stomach. Moreover, he is likely to be staggering with fatigue after a nonstop day in quest of fun. These two elements alone leave the body open to a swift and dramatic assault by alcohol. In addition the body chemistry at that time of day is characterized by low blood sugar levels, a situation that makes the central nervous system all the more susceptible. A man who can drink four Scotches-on-the-rocks after a good meal with only a pleasant mellowing effect may be blasted before dinner by two martinis.

This is how alcohol takes people by surprise. Most likely to overshoot are those who drink only on weekends and lack experience to gauge their capacities at various times of day. In their Sunday-morning agony they often blame it all on the type of drink they had and swear never to approach that particular mixture again. The martini, for example, often bears blame of this sort. It is thought to be an enormously potent drink with a sneaky delayed-action effect. It does indeed have a faintly sinister appearance. But actually it is no more potent than any other liquid of like alcoholic content. Its reputation comes mainly from the time of day at which it is usually injected into the defenseless bloodstream.

The sociability peak of a large gathering always comes just before massive overshooting begins to be evident. It comes when perhaps half the guests are just loose enough to create an atmosphere of faintly giddy gaiety. Those who aren't yet that loose are drawn into the spirit of things. Those who have already overshot are controlled by the dominant emotional tone which doesn't yet grant unlimited license. The peak passes when the majority have overshot. Then some grow loud, some grow clumsily flirtatious, some grow tired and some grow sick. Many do and say things at which they will be aghast tomorrow morning. The tensions between people are now so thoroughly anesthetized that no further reactions take place.

Eventually the majority of the guests drift away, and only ten or so remain. Now the post-party party is in session. There is almost always such a minor party after a major one. Sometimes the hostess plans it, inviting "special friends" to stay for supper or—in the case of a night drinking party—for a midnight snack or breakfast. Most often it just happens. The Chicago partygoers felt the post-party party is "for those whose needs have not been met." Some haven't drunk deeply enough of sociability, perhaps, and still feel a little lonesome. Others don't feel they've shone brightly enough and hope now for a last chance. And possibly some feel a need to taper off from the intense flow of affection they've just experienced, as from a drug. They are reluctant to quit cold turkey and walk out into the lonely night. The post-party party, always quiet, always low-keyed, offers a less intense kind of sociability on which to effect the needed tapering off. To use another analogy, it might be called a decompression party.

The dozen burnt-out weekenders huddle around a coffee table and talk desultorily, allowing long silences to fall. Some silences are louder than others. Those at a decompression party are typically quiet. They are among the few silences the likeables find tolerable.

The Chicago partygoers concluded there are three things weekenders hope to get from parties. One is a sense of solidarity, a demonstration that a group exists and that each is included in it. Another is a sense of festivity or gaiety. That is, the solidarity must be of the fun-filled rather than solemn variety, in keeping with the weekend mood. The third element is intimacy, a feeling of getting close to people. This is probably the most elusive of the three elements and the hardest to summon up. It is characteristically the main goal of small parties.

The intimacy expected of the small gathering dictates that the personalities of those invited must be assessed with care. Host and hostess worry about who will "go" with whom. Often they try to dilute the personal interaction by asking guests to play bridge or some other game. This at least insures that the party members will have something to do when they can't think of anything to talk about. But the game may be relied upon too heavily. It may become a crutch for personalities afraid to trust their own strength. Then little or no interaction takes place, and the party becomes merely a mechanical drill on a code of rules written by Charles Goren or a games manufacturer. Guests are likely to go home feeling neither success nor failure but emptiness, like a ball player who works himself up to a high pitch of competitive zeal and finds the game postponed.

The need for careful personality picking is made more acute by the fact that the typical small weekend party is leaderless. The modern weekend host and hostess simply initiate the gathering, provide the meeting place and the food and drink, and perhaps state a general agenda. Then they efface themselves. They play no stronger a role in steering the group, and may deliberately play a lesser role, than the guests.

Partygoers earlier in this century would have been baffled by such unhostlike behavior. In those days the host considered his living room a forum over which he presided. He led the conversations, sometimes even announcing in a rather formal way what he felt could profitably be talked about. "I'd like to know how all of you feel about morality in the modern novel," he'd say as he took his chair by the fireplace. Throughout the evening he and often his wife solicitously watched over their guests. They carefully drew out silent members, tactfully shut up those who were talking too much.

The business-oriented parties of the workweek are also likely to be dominated by strong hosts. Such a party may be run by an executive or a group of executives who have been designated as its leaders. Their job is to keep the party going and make announcements or otherwise fulfill the purpose of the gathering. They can't let it become a mere likeability exchange. The traditional and terrifying dinner with the boss is also likely to be strongly led. The boss may try to be one of the boys, but nobody ever forgets who he really is.

But the weekend host and hostess are reluctant to take on such a role. They want affection as much as does any of their guests. They want to be included in the group, not placed over it or to one side, beyond the exchange of liking.

If you were able to turn invisible and visit small Saturday-night parties of people you didn't know, you would find it hard to guess who were the actual host and hostess in many cases. Even when somebody got up to pass the peanuts, mix drinks or wipe a spill off the coffee table, you still couldn't be sure. Surrogate hosting includes jobs such as these. At a dinner party it may even include clearing the table and whipping the cream for dessert. The Chicago partygoers coded 2,000 "sociable episodes" on IBM cards. Of all male behavior at parties only 10 per cent could be called hosting or surrogate hosting, and of all female behavior, only 9.9 per cent. In your attempt to pick out the host or hostess, you'd find nine-tenths of all that happened at a party gave you no clues. The remaining tenth would only confuse you.

Some scientists have tried to find out what happens in leaderless groups such as these. One is Dr. Robert F. Bales, Harvard University psychologist. Under his supervision Harvard some years ago set up a Social Relations Laboratory in which small groups are studied by observers looking through one-way glass. Each group is given a problem to solve, but it isn't given a leader or any other help. The torments and triumphs of the various group members are recorded by means of a numerical code.

These are not sociability groups, of course. Each group has a clearly stated problem and must solve it. A sociability group has a problem but seldom knows precisely what it is. Despite this difference the Harvard groups provide some odd little insights into the dynamics of a small weekend party. In particular they show some of the ways in which various kinds of people reach out for human contact in small groups.

Dr. Bales and another Harvard psychologist, Dr. Edgar Borgatta, classified group members broadly according to four elements in the personality of each: how other members rated him on leadership, how he rated himself, how they rated him on popularity and how popular he thought he was. Of course there are many possible grades of leadership and popularity, but for simplicity Drs. Bales and Borgatta boiled all the possibilities down to a plain plus or minus (above median or below median) in each case. Thus a member either was considered a good leader or wasn't. He either thought he was or didn't. Thus classified, 125 people were divided into small groups, the groups were assigned problems and the psychologists watched to see what would happen.

Which type of member did the most talking? In a report in the *Journal of Social Psychology* Drs. Bales and Borgatta identify him as the member whom others consider a good leader and who so considers himself, but who mistakenly thinks himself popular. Here is a recognizable weekend type: the notorious Life of the Party. He tells jokes, suggests games, turns on the phonograph and dances with the hostess. The other guests reluctantly admire him and may be grateful to him in the party's early faltering stages. But as the evening wears on and alcohol releases their own pent-up wit, they begin to wish he would pipe down. He irritates them but never seems to sense it. He shows tension less often than any other member.

In ninety-six minutes of group sessions at Harvard the average member of this type initiated 583 acts or remarks. That's a lot of talking for an hour and a half. No other type of member even approached it. And 78 per cent of all this powerful member's furious activity consisted in giving opinions or orientation. No other member had that much nerve. Dr. Bales calls this general type of member the Task Specialist. His consuming interest is to get the job done, and he fails either to sense or to sympathize with any emotional damage other members may suffer along the way. That's why he is unpopular, and he gets demonstrably more so as the sessions progress.

Thus it is with the Life of the Party. He wants high sociability and goes after it with single-minded ferocity. Perhaps he craves affection more intensely than other weekenders and hopes by his actions to become the center of liking in the group. Quite often the Life is a man who spends the workweek hidden in some obscure corporate corner, frustrated by his inability to command people's attention. Most metropolitans suffer from workweek feelings of anonymity but the Life seems more than normally troubled. The weekend gives him his chance to be somebody.

The second most active group member is another type who assesses himself wrongly but in a rather charming way. This is the member whom the others consider both likeable and a good leader, and who knows he's likeable but wrongly judges himself a poor leader. His average total of acts in an hour and a half is 499, against the Life's 583. He spends far less of his time trying to lead the group. He spends 16 per cent of it (against the Life's 7 per cent) in what the Harvard scientists call positive reaction—laughing, agreeing, showing solidarity and affection. His major function in the group is to smooth feathers ruffled by the Life. His attention is on the people rather than the task. Dr. Bales calls this general breed of member the Social Specialist.

It is advisable to invite the Social Specialist to any party that includes a Life. Often he comes automatically, for he is likely to be the Life's husband or (more commonly) wife. Through long experience she has learned to take on the role of smoother and healer in her husband's violent wake. She holds him in check when he begins to get out of control. When the other guests lack the nerve, she will disagree with him. The Harvard records show she disagrees more often than any other member, usually with the Life and often for the other members' sake. She is fine-tuned to the shifting moods around her. She knows when the others don't want to play Password and, good-humoredly if possible, removes pencil and paper from the Life's eager, quivering hands.

It may be that the Social Specialist's need for affection is as great as the Life's, but she seems more quietly sure she deserves it. She obviously enjoys being popular. What she doesn't seem to realize is that, in the lonely metropolitan society and particularly on weekends, popularity itself is a kind of leadership.

At the lower end of the scale sits a very quiet member. This is the amiably mousey man or woman whom nobody considers much of a leader and who agrees, but who wrongly believes he isn't well liked. The others like him fine. Perhaps they like him because of his very quietness. His acts in the Harvard sessions totalled only 356. Possibly the others enjoy his company because he represents no kind of sociable competition. It is refreshing to be with somebody who isn't striving for popularity.

Or maybe the others like the Mouse because he has never

given them a reason not to. He has never topped their jokes with better ones of his own. He has never avoided their table at the club because he has never joined the club. The Mouse doesn't make the scene much anywhere around town. He has never excluded anybody from his cocktail parties because he has never given any cocktail parties. He doesn't believe enough people would bother to come if he did.

Actually in this last belief he may be correct. Though the Mouse is liked, he isn't popular in the weekend sense of the word. The weekenders don't feel impelled to go out of their way to smile at him. When he's around, they like him. When he isn't, they forget all about him.

It is hard to say how much all this troubles the Mouse. He may be one of Riesman's inner-directed people, who carry their justifications within them instead of shaping each act for its effect on other people. The Mouse seems content with a few friends and shows little need to have or display a large sociable circle. But he may sometimes wonder whether his system of values is all wrong. Most of the others around him obviously consider it wrong. It is hard to live in a society and not subscribe to its ways of thinking. This could cause inner conflict that might be very painful to the Mouse. The Harvard records show he is among the most tense of all members.

The most tense member is a strangely deluded one. This is the individual whom the others consider a good leader but don't find particularly likeable, and who sizes himself up incorrectly on both counts. Almost 9 per cent of his activity consists in showing tension (against 1.6 per cent for the peculiarly insensitive Life). On the weekend scene this could be the well-known Organizer, often a woman, who by default rises to the chairmanships of committees, fund drives and clubs. She is officious and a bustler. Because other people shun these thankless chairmanships, she wins them easily, erroneously believing she wins them because she is popular. She has a hard time getting people on her committees to do what they're supposed to do, and this may make her feel she isn't a good leader. Actually people know the jobs she does must be done and are glad she is doing them. Though they don't like her much, they are glad to hand her the burden of leadership.

The Organizer is typically a tense individual. At an intimate Saturday night party she may grow more tense as alcohol lets people show more of their feelings. The Organizer finds few expressions of affection coming her way. The Life doesn't pull her from her chair to dance. Nobody makes witty remarks about her sex life. At such times her self-assessment argues with observable fact. To reassure herself she goes to church next morning and rounds up people for a committee to decide what to give the minister for his birthday.

It would be ridiculous to say the weekenders don't enjoy themselves at their popularity exchanges. Often they do. There come moments when they feel warmly enclosed in the group.

They laugh with genuine gaiety. They feel honest liking for one another. Often with the help of alcohol, the party does for them what they came hoping it would do.

But the Chicago researchers found it "noteworthy . . . how seldom partygoers in our observation went expecting a good time." The compulsion toward gay sociability often trips over its own ponderous feet. The weekenders want so badly to relax and love each other that they grow tense and afraid of each other instead. It would be unduly pessimistic of them to go to every weekend gathering with the glum foreboding that precedes a dental visit, but they are strongly aware it is possible to go to a party and wish one hadn't. On the other hand, they are also aware that whenever they don't go to a party they wish they had.

7. The Sin Symbolists

AN OBSERVANT BELLHOP at the Caribe Hilton Hotel in San Juan, Puerto Rico, told a strange little tale about an October weekend. The tale is either happy or sad, depending on the point of view. On a Friday night a mid-thirtyish couple flew in from Florida and registered for a two-day stay. While escorting them to their room, the bellhop noticed signs of nervousness between them. One of their suitcases had initials on it which didn't match the name they had given when registering as Mr. and Mrs. While the bellhop was showing the man how to operate various gadgets, the woman stood by the bed and twisted her fingers in apparent agitation. The man gave the bellhop an unusually large tip. The bellhop went back to the lobby grinning to himself.

Partly because of the big tip and partly out of ordinary human curiosity, the bellhop kept an eye on the couple and their weekend adventure. He saw them from time to time on Saturday, sometimes with a group of sociables they'd evidently met at the beach but most often alone. They ate in quiet corners and walked hand-in-hand. They seemed to be enjoying an idyllic interlude from whatever lives they led on the mainland. The bellhop wondered whether they were married to other spouses or whether one or both were single. Once he was able to get close enough to see the woman wore no wedding ring.

On Sunday afternoon he carried their suitcases down to the lobby and helped them check out. They seemed tired and pensive, no longer nervous, apparently reluctant to go back to the workday world which lacked room for their love. The bellhop felt a touch of sadness. But then the woman said something that gave him his biggest surprise of the weekend.

She turned to the man and said, "We'd better get some seashell beads or something for the kids."

She said it in the calm familiar tone of wife to husband. And when the startled bellhop looked at her left hand, he saw a golden ring.

Why were this man and wife pretending to be partners in sin? Why the masquerade—the wedding ring removed, the assumed name or assumed suitcase, the large guilt-edged tip? They were merely playing an elaborate version of a game that is played everywhere on weekends by people married and single. They were seeking a weekend escape from the humdrum, and as a symbol of this escape they were using the idea or ideal of sin.

Sin as an abstraction is viewed with ambivalent feelings by the modern metropolitan society. Everybody knows he should hate and shun it because he has been so taught since childhood. Yet it appears to offer certain qualities of feeling that the typical metropolitan may think are missing from his workday life.

For one thing, sin has a glamorous exciting sound to those who have felt themselves on a treadmill all week. In the white-collar society there aren't many jobs that normally yield adventure. Housewives are especially troubled by boredom, notably the college-educated who feel their talents are shamefully wasted amid dishes, diapers and dust mops. The weekend for many represents the week's single big opportunity for release from the day-after-dayness of it all. It offers a chance to escape those aspects of oneself and one's life that sometimes grow tiresome, all the attributes of middle-class respectability that are needled by young writers in undergraduate literary magazines.

The idea of sin expresses this escape succinctly and vibrantly.

Our society for many decades has harbored a secret smile for naughtiness in general. The expression "goody-goody" refers to a child, most often a boy, who obeys all the rules all the time. We like to hear of a boy who obeys the big rules but sometimes breaks the little ones. A father may roar with anguish when he finds his son fishing in a neighbor's goldfish pond but later will tell the story with ill-concealed pride. He is likely to be expressing his own feeling of being caught in an immense web of laws and rules and his admiration for anybody who has the guts occasionally to break free. The complicated metropolitan world needs a library full of rules to ward off chaos, and most metropolitans abide by the rules most of the time. But sometimes the rules chafe. The spirit feels stifled. There are Federal and state laws, local ordinances, company policy and the whole massive code of unwritten rules by which metropolitans live together in irritable peace. George Orwell in *1984* expressed modern man's feeling of belonging to somebody other than himself and his suspicion that it is all getting worse. The weekend gives him a chance to break the rules a little, feel slightly naughty and know that he belongs to himself after all. Sin is the handiest, most obvious and usually least dangerous way to accomplish this.

In fact it might be said that the idea of sin is the most forceful expression of the weekend frame of mind. It would be hard to think of anything less like the work ethic than the ideal of sin, with its spirit of adventurous enjoyment and its wide-open license. In being or pretending to be sinful, the weekenders are trying to get as far from work as possible.

It isn't necessary of course to engage in full-scale acts of sin in order to feel or look sinful. The common brand of weekend rule breaking is not actually sin itself but rather the symbol of it. The weekenders as a breed are not sinners but sin symbolists. Their infractions of the rules are most often minor. Like the couple at the Caribe Hilton they gain some of the emotional values of an escape from the humdrum without the risk that a real escape would entail.

Sin symbolism comes in many shapes. Women on weekends wear perfume with names like Desire and My Sin. Whether these truly have an aphrodisiac effect on the human male is not established, but that doesn't matter. It is the name that counts. The name reflects the attitude of the wearer. These are weekend perfumes, to be worn by women who wish to be other than housewives, office help or schoolteachers. In the same way cocktail and after-five dresses for most women are for weekends. They reveal more shoulder, collarbone and sternum than clothes normally worn on workdays by either career women or housewives. Merchants in advertising such garments pluck their copy from the fringes of pornography. The dresses are "suggestive," "provocative," "daring" and "wicked." As a woman changes into such a dress on Saturday night, she changes her outlook and personality.

Thus starts the fun. There was a time when making casual passes at another man's girl friend, wife or sister invited anger or, at best, considerable grumpiness. The male weekender today is not only permitted but encouraged to do and say things over which men once dueled to the death. At parties he often adopts a ponderously lascivious manner. The women he accosts respond delightedly. Though they may be proper and most respectable people during the workweek, on weekends they like to look and feel slightly disreputable.

Only slightly, as a rule. Just enough to get the feeling of gay disobedience. A man at a party meets a woman not his wife. Both have had a drink or two and are feeling sociable. They converse alone. As long as they are alone, the spice of sin doesn't enter their conversation, for then it would be too close to the real thing. But when others join them, they are at liberty to symbolize. "What are you two doing over here in the dark?" somebody asks with a lewd grin. The woman presses her cheek to the man's and says, "None of your business." Actually they were talking about the library fund drive. But now the game is on. The man puts his arm about his symbolic paramour's waist and makes a remark about bedrooms or bushes.

Then they stand flatfooted. The game has gone as far as it can go. Neither the man nor the woman, nor the onlookers, believe for a moment that anything other than symbolism is afoot. Yet nobody wants to admit in words that the whole thing was just a sham. All want to preserve the disreputable mood. For a while they grin at each other awkwardly. Then the man tells the woman he'll see her later and the episode ends. But the mood lingers on.

One of the most common forms of symbolism is the sex joke. The prepackaged or heat-and-serve witticism is common conversational fare throughout the middle classes on weekends today. Laboring-class people tend to use manufactured jokes less often. They are more likely to depend on their own wit. Upper-class people and those with intellectual pretensions as a rule disdain packaged jokes as conversational crutches, useful only to the dim-witted. But most weekender groups use them liberally.

In the lower strata of the middle class the jokes are generally quite mild. Typically the punch line is so devised that the sinful situation or conclusion will be conceived in the listener's own busy mind. In the higher strata the jokes are more daring and more often told by women. High-voltage words are used as freely as in the works of young novelists. Indeed, some jokes are constructed for the sole purpose of pronouncing a single magnificent word. Some seem funnier after a few drinks than when reviewed in a sober hour, and many a sociable has sat on the edge of his bed in the clear bright light of Sunday morning and thought, gently quivering, "O Lord, did I really tell *that* one?" Some suddenly seem less funny halfway through the telling, as the raconteur realizes to his horror that his hearers are not prepared for so robust a brand of symbolism. A strained laugh follows the disastrous punch line. The laugh fades to a whisper and drifts away into infinity. For a few moments after that the ear can sometimes detect a faint whistling sound as the raconteur folds himself up like an accordion.

Packaged jokes are used in a variety of ways. Often their advent signals a feeling that sociability or the sinful mood, or both, haven't grown intense enough or have begun to dim. The tellers are trying to light an emotional fire. At other times a sinful story may be told by someone who feels he has failed in other ways that evening. He hasn't sin-symbolized enough, or he hasn't been reassured enough about his likeability. The manufactured joke temporarily gives him the center of the stage. "Ever hear the story about the blue alligator in the laundromat?" he asks. A hush falls on the group. Everybody leans forward with faintly lustful expectation. The storyteller now has his chance to symbolize sin, albeit in an indirect and impersonal way. If the joke succeeds, he enjoys the experience. He has been naughty and has got away without a spanking.

Among the least subtle forms of sin symbolism is that which springs up on a college campus on weekends. Some forty years ago a book reviewer, taking a dig at F. Scott Fitzgerald, noted that college students have a habit of "not kissing but telling anyway." The trait is in evidence all through the academic week, but on weekends it sometimes becomes the dominant fact of campus life. This is particularly true at noncoeducational colleges, where the ordinary workweek strictures against whooping it up are further enforced by the absence of the opposite sex.

A proctor at Princeton University, charged with maintaining weekend decorum among the ivied walls, was telling about his early experiences with the young male metropolitans and their dates. It has long been the university's policy to enforce a curfew on football and party weekends. All lady guests are supposed to be out of the dormitory rooms after a certain hour, which over the years has varied from seven o'clock to midnight, depending on the apparent trustworthiness of the undergraduate body that year and the wish of university officials to be good pals. This curfew is a rich source of sin symbolism.

"There was one group of boys who always made a lot of noise about sex," the proctor reminisced. "I kept hearing campus rumors about how they'd had girls in their rooms after the curfew. One big party weekend I decided to watch them." He stood in the dark near their dormitory and watched a large alcohol-fueled popularity exchange that was visible through a second-floor window. When the curfew hour approached, he heard an alarm clock ring loudly next to the window. This was followed by shouts and shrieks of glee, then by dead silence. The lights were turned low. The shades were drawn.

"I waited about twenty minutes but none of the girls left the dorm," said the proctor. "Then I went in and walked up the stairs. The door of the room was ajar and I walked in."

The sinful scene that greeted him was as follows. The young men and women were sitting in chairs and on the floor. A few of the men had their arms about girls' shoulders, but this was the only circumstance remotely connected with sin. The group was watching a home movie of somebody's trip to Bermuda.

The proctor herded the girls out of the building and prepared to leave himself. One of the young men accosted him at the door. "Aren't you going to report us?" the young man asked.

The proctor realized to his surprise that there was a distinct note of regret in the question. "The boy *wanted* to be reported," he said later. "And so did the others. They wanted the whole college to think they'd had an orgy. They wanted me to do their bragging for them."

In a way sin symbolism might be thought of as simply an extension of the fun mystique. Sin is perhaps the most visible kind of fun. The sinner doesn't need to prove to anybody that he is having fun. Everybody is aware of it, once the knowledge gets out that he has achieved or seemed to achieve sin. He isn't depressed, repressed, inhibited or any of those things. He is generally agreed to be really living. He has escaped the work ethic and achieved a well-rounded, emotionally successful life.

People who seek weekend contentment by climbing mountains, jumping out of airplanes with parachutes, flying kites and raising primroses sometimes have a hard time convincing others this is fun. The same difficulty even faces some more common kinds of weekenders. Golfers are pincushions for the barbed wit of nongolfers. Suburban gardeners and weekend farmers are roundly jeered at every Monday morning by those who have stayed in the city. It is not easy to describe the quality of an enjoyment precisely. Ben Hogan can write books telling us how to hold our woods and irons, but he can't tell us how to enjoy it.

The sinner or sin symbolist escapes all this difficulty. Sexual enjoyment is tangible, specific and almost universally understood. It is doubtful that anybody ever asked of a sinner, "What on earth does he *get* out of it?"

In contrast to symbolism, real sin requires effort, carries great risk and involves an often painful break with inbred patterns of morality. Despite these discouragements it, too, raises its head on weekends. Sometimes it comes into evidence as a result of symbolism that has gone out of control and run wild. Sometimes it arrives all by itself.

Sin isn't confined to weekends of course. But it is more likely to appear on a weekend than on any weekday. The mood of the weekend is more receptive to it. The psychoanalyst S. Ferenczi, observer of the Sunday neurosis, noted that people on weekends are less tightly shackled by traditional thou-shalt-nots. Some are frightened by this extra freedom, some welcome it and some use it for purposes of sin. Dr. Jean Rosenbaum, the Detroit psychiatrist who is among leading modern-day students of the weekend mind, likes to refer to the phenomenon in terms of regression—a backtracking toward childhood. People on weekends, like children, tend to give way to their impulses instead of fighting themselves as they must do all week.

"People loosen up on weekends," he says. He tells of a patient he once had who was never able to talk freely on workdays. The analytic situation requires a breaking down of the patient's reticence in the doctor's presence. The patient must be able to talk of things he may never have mentioned to anybody else. This particular man couldn't achieve the needed loosening until the weekend when his hopes, fears and worries poured out of him in a torrent. He could speak of his sexual and other problems with little apparent embarrassment.

The extent of weekend sin is hard to gauge accurately. Statistical evidence is scarce. A sociologist once proposed to arrive at some sort of measurement by gathering data on what he called "brief stays" at motels. A brief stay is one in which a man and woman register as married, occupy a room or cabin for only an hour or two and then depart. There could be many reasons for such behavior, but sin is undoubtedly the most common one.

Unfortunately the sociologist wasn't able to get enough solid data on this intriguing custom. Motel owners were reluctant to give out the needed information, even those whose records revealed it in a systematic way. It isn't the fault of a motel or hotel when people use the premises for sin, for the management can't sensibly require every couple to produce a marriage license. Still the motel industry is anxious to avoid the reputation of catering to sin.

All the same, the sociologist came away with the impression that brief stays are typically a Saturday-night phenomenon. In fact he told me of one rather unkempt establishment that offers a cut rate for any stay short enough to permit renting the same cabin again that same night. Weedy and moribund through the workweek, this particular motel thrives lustily on the weekend.

If brief stays are indeed confined largely to the weekend, this indicates how different the weekend mood is from that of the workweek. If there were no difference in mood, people would be as likely to sin on Wednesday night after work as on Saturday night. But Wednesday night is not a sinner's night. Saturday night is.

Another indication of the difference in mood shows up in records dealing with crimes of passion. These are typically weekend crimes. For example, look into the files of the Cincinnati Division of Police, which keeps highly detailed crime tabulations. Take the year 1961. For simplicity compare Saturday with a single weekday, say Wednesday. Which is the most passionate day?

There were 58 criminal homicides committed in Cincinnati in 1961. Of these, 8 were committed on Wednesdays and 14 on Saturdays. Seven women or girls were forcibly raped on Wednesdays, but nearly three times as many—20—were attacked on Saturdays. There were 33 cases of aggravated assault on Wednesdays and 91 on Saturdays—again, almost three times as many.

This is startling evidence, but it isn't quite complete. For the greater amount of Saturday passion could indicate simply that people have more free time on Saturdays. People with regular jobs would have less opportunity to murder, rape or assault during the workweek. Perhaps their passions burn as high on Wednesdays, but work requirements prevent the passions' being expressed.

This might be true if the crimes were committed during the day. They aren't. Like brief motel stays, crimes of passion are characteristically activities of the night. The Los Angeles Police Department, which also keeps detailed records, finds that by far the greatest number of violent crimes occur on Friday and Saturday nights after seven o'clock. These are crimes that could just as easily be committed on Wednesday nights. But they aren't. People aren't in the same mood then.

The weekend is the time for letting go, living life to its fullest—the time of passion. It is also the time for coeducational drinking. When alcohol mixes with a general wish to obey impulses, sin is a predictable result.

It is more often accidental than soberly premeditated. Of course there are some weekender groups in which it is quite cold-bloodedly planned. There are undress parties among the single, latchkey and novelty parties among the married. Around San Bernardino, California, police in 1962 broke up a highly organized weekend mate-swapping club of more than fifteen couples. But none of this could be called typical weekend behavior.

It sometimes seems more widespread than it probably is because we hear so much about it. It makes news. Sometimes it is made as news. An editor calls in a reporter and asks for a shocking report on cocktail communities, sin circles or whatever he chooses to call his largely imaginary orgy clubs. The reporter, needing to earn a living, rounds up some startling case histories. This is legitimate. But what the reporter has in his notes is then presented as typical, when in fact there is no proof that it is. This is not legitimate.

People like to think there are orgy clubs all over town. The imagined existence of some nearby Sodom makes stimulating conversation. Moreover it provides a basis of weekend sin symbolism. A man is known by the company he keeps, and weekenders sometimes like to pretend they are acquainted with far-gone sinners. "When I first moved into this town I met a girl who gave me the lowdown on everybody," a young wife told me. "She warned me about a 'fast crowd' I was likely to meet

some weekend and went through all the rumors about this
crowd. She scared me. I wondered what kind of place we'd
moved into. Well, since then I've met the 'fast crowd' and been
to some of their parties. They're just ordinary people." The
informant was just a symbolist. And it is likely that of all the
fast crowds that are said to exist in city and suburb, at least
half are a good deal slower than reported.

Most often the weekend sinner slides into sin gradually and
without having planned it, impelled as much by weekend social
pressures as by his own volition. He indulges in symbolism
and sticks with it even when it becomes too intense for his
taste. He doesn't want to be called a prude. Among the weekenders this is as bad as being thought funless. Meanwhile he
has been drinking. Eventually he works himself into a state in
which symbolism can arouse his passions when it was intended
only to represent them.

A young married woman told of an alcohol feast in which
this process took place. It was a large noisy affair and started
like many weekend parties with mild symbolism which ripened.
First there were just words: ribald jokes and adventurous
remarks. Then there was the laying on of hands. Men and
women hugged waists, patted cheeks, stroked backs of necks
and twined fingers. Then there was a flurry of kissing. Whether
this represents a crossing of the borderline between symbolism
and sin is a matter of personal interpretation. The young
woman (I will call her Mary) felt the line had been crossed.
But she allowed herself to be kissed a few times. "I didn't want
to be a killjoy," she explained.

Now the party began to expand into unused rooms. Couples
would disappear from the living room and reappear ten or
fifteen minutes later, looking rumpled. Mary wasn't sure
whether they had committed full-dress adultery, merely petted
or just talked about the PTA. The loud talk suggested adultery,
but this might have been only symbolism. Mary had no way of
knowing. Her guess was that adultery was committed or at

least attempted by some of the couples. Probably she was right. This may not have been the sinners' plan as they left the living room. Most may have thought they'd only pet for a while and return to the party in symbolic triumph. But one thing leads to another, and symbolism when allowed to go this far can't always be halted at will.

Mary now badly wanted to go home and sensed her husband did too. Unfortunately the hostess had previously invited her to stay for the post-party party. If the apparent sin were indeed only symbolism, to leave now would seem "hopelessly middle class," as Mary put it. Middle-class weekenders hate to be called middle class. But if the sin were real, to stay could be risky. Mary feared she might have to be rude to some of the men. She also feared she might not have the resistance to be rude enough.

She and her husband solved the problem by leaving the party without saying good-bye. Nobody seemed sober enough to notice. Next day Mary phoned the hostess and apologized, giving as her excuse a migraine headache. The hostess at the time had two migraine headaches, one on each side. She said she understood.

In telling this story Mary seemed shocked not at the idea of sin itself but at the idea of performing it thus almost in public. Public sin and its cousin, symbolism, are of course methods of gaining weekend status. The sinner makes himself seem high-fun.

If this seems to be a rather odd use of sex, consider its use by our national folk heros and heroines, the movie folk. The old Hollywood days of mutiple divorces are apparently on the wane. Now the bright young star avoids marriage. Instead he and his mistress go to live on an island in the Mediterranean, a villa in Spain or a large metropolitan hotel. Melina Mercouri and Jules Dassin, Romy Schneider and the French actor she calls her "engaged husband," Elizabeth Taylor and Richard Burton: these are examples of love affairs conducted in public.

Elsa Martinelli once granted *Esquire* an entire interview to explain her living arrangement with a photographer named Willy. Such arrangements are conducted not only openly but with great pride. Look at us, the stars seem to say. We are emancipated moderns, free of the old prudish inhibitions. We really know how to live! Movie publicity agents are aware of the allure this has for the ordinary American in search of the good life. It sometimes seems the Mediterranean must be a-froth with publicity men hunting islands for their clients' gracious sinning. I was buttonholed once by an agent who wanted me to write a magazine article about his client, an obscure TV actress, and her "life outlook." She lived with an equally obscure actor. When I told the agent I doubted if anybody would care much, he seemed ready to burst into tears. "But they aren't married!" he cried. "Don't you see? They aren't married!"

Sin can't always be conducted in public, of course, particularly by married people. The weekend of secret sin is an entity well known to marriage counselors and psychiatrists. In this case the sinner is often in search of a subtle ingredient that is missing in visible sin and symbolism. The ingredient is an aura of gentleness or sweetness. Instead of emphasizing the sensual aspects of sin, as the symbolists do, the secret weekend sinner is likely to put at least as much emphasis on the ethereal. He envisions an idyllic period of pure love. He may picture himself and his love romping in sunlit water by day, later walking hand-in-hand through misty twilight and still later watching clouds sail past the moon. He hopes it won't rain.

This kind of idyll can be attempted during the workweek, too. But it represents a dream characteristic of the weekend. It is entirely in keeping with the weekend goal of a rich full life, a mostly tranquil time punctuated by intense joyful experiences. In any case the workweek doesn't easily yield time enough for such an interlude. One thing no idyll can tolerate is a sense of hurry.

A psychiatrist told of a weekend of secret sin that took place in 1961. His patient was a single woman in her late twenties who was suffering great unhappiness over a love affair with a married man. She worked as a secretary in a large company. He was an executive in the same company, and they believed themselves to have fallen in love. Their affair was conducted largely by skulking about the city at lunch hour, looking for restaurants not likely to be frequented by those who knew them. Occasionally the executive was able to make excuses to his wife and visit the young woman in her apartment. But the hurry and furtiveness of all this exuded a sordid air that was intolerable to both sinners. Eventually they looked to the weekend for the cleansing and sweetening effect they felt their affair needed.

The executive reserved a room in a hotel at a small, obscure mountain lake resort. He told his wife he was off on a business trip. The plan was for him and the young woman to fly separately to a city near the resort and meet at the airport, whence they would complete the journey together in a rented car. Unfortunately the executive ran into urgent business problems on Friday afternoon and missed his plane. By the time he arrived at the contact point, the secretary had spent almost three hours wandering morosely about the airport and was awash with coffee, tired, nervous and quite put out. The executive was even more put out. He felt she should understand his lateness since she worked for the same company and knew its sometimes harsh requirements. In fact, work had impinged on a weekend which they'd thought was going to be their own. But neither saw things in this detached way. They drove to the resort in tense silence.

The managers of obscure resort hotels are aware of the uses to which their premises are sometimes put, but they are no more nosy than anybody else. Still the secretary was certain the manager and his entire staff guessed her situation as soon as she entered the hotel lobby. She burned with shame when the executive registered her as his wife. She felt the whole hotel would be snickering at her all weekend and was sure she wouldn't be able to make herself leave her room. Sadly she realized the weekend wasn't going to provide a release from furtiveness. Nor could it cleanse the stain of sordidness. These sprang from her own feelings of guilt, and guilt can't be erased by a mere change of scenery or exposure to mountain air, pine trees and moonlight.

It rained next day anyway. When the rain stopped in the evening, the two lovers attempted an idyllic walk along the lakeshore. But there is hardly anything damper than a lake-shore after rainfall. Moreover the executive thought he saw poison ivy along the footpath. He was highly susceptible, he said. He wondered how he would explain to his wife if he returned home with his legs blistered. Perhaps he could say he'd played business golf. He began mumbling a roll call of distant friends who, if necessary, would swear they'd spent the day with him on the links.

Next morning the executive examined his legs apprehensively. To his horror he found them covered with bumplets in rows and patches, the early signs of what promised to be a massive ivy attack. His legs instantly began to itch intolerably, but this was nothing compared to the itching of both sinners' consciences. They returned to metropolia unhappy and disillusioned, wondering if they were still in love or indeed had ever been. The executive's legs were smeared with pink salve. No drugstore on earth sold a salve for their other complaints.

In 1962 a prominent California marriage counselor, being interviewed on television by Art Linkletter, gave his view that the large amount of leisure time we enjoy every week is a threat to the institution of marriage. People become bored with all this idleness, he said. In search of stimulation they play with alcohol and sex, and as a result marriages break up. The view was not his alone but has been voiced quite often in the past ten years. If this is true, we have much to fear from the three-day weekend which may arrive in some of our lifetimes.

But there is no trustworthy evidence that it is true. The typical weekend isn't a period of idleness. For most people the problem is too little free time, not too much. The weekend is too full of a number of things, and sin is but one of them. If people on weekends do turn to sin out of boredom, it is likely to be either a boredom with their spouses or a boredom with the monotony of the metropolitan workweek. None of this has much to do with the kind of boredom the marriage counselor meant, the yawning kind that comes from a long period of nothing to do.

It is true a greater amount of sinning apparently occurs on the weekend than in the workweek. But the weekend's sinful reputation probably comes largely from the vast amount of symbolizing that goes on. There is sex in the air everywhere on Saturday night, but most of it seems to stay in the air. If the divorce rate is an indication (it may not be an accurate one), most people take marriage about as seriously today as they did forty years ago when relatively few enjoyed a two-day weekend. Today they just talk more about sin.

If there is any kind of worsening national sex problem, the factual evidence is that it exists mostly among the young and single. A genuine change in moral standards governing the single seems to be taking place. Helen Gurley Brown in her 1962 book *Sex and the Single Girl* became a spokesman for the new ways of thinking. She advanced the view that sex is a weapon which the single girl may use without guilt to make her way in the competitive metropolitan society. Large numbers of single girls have adopted this viewpoint in recent decades, some of them to their eternal regret. According to the National Offices of Vital Statistics the birth rate of illegitimate children has tripled in the last twenty years. There were seven live births among every 1,000 unmarried women in 1940, and twenty-one in 1958. The largest numbers of such births always occur among teen-age girls and those in their early twenties. But the biggest percentage increase since 1940 has been among young adult women aged twenty-five to thirty-nine, Helen Gurley Brown's main audience.

For the single girl with the sex-as-a-weapon philosophy the weekend may become more important in terms of long-range goals than her workweek job. Sad to say, a girl's chances of success in a working career are usually less good than those of a man with the same qualifications. On weekends she seeks to make up for the handicap by using sex. She can use it to win a carefully chosen husband, says Mrs. Brown, or a coveted job or assignment, or just "gifts and money." On Saturday at a ski lodge, beach or alcohol feast she wields considerably more power than she did on Friday at her desk. In her circles weekend activities may be strongly dominated by sin, not symbolism.

Even so there is no reason to condemn leisure time. It is not the long stretch of workless time itself that most often causes sin but the attitudes of people toward the weekend and the needs and dreams they bring to it from the workweek. If it develops that large numbers of people are getting themselves into trouble over weekend sin, it will be necessary to ask questions about many aspects of the metropolitan society, not just the society's time away from work. It will be useful at the same time to think of all the magnificent things that can be done with two days off.

The weekend is like a big red apple. Some would eat it too fast and get indigestion. But it is still a lovely apple.

8. Weekend Worshipers

A Protestant minister gazed pensively into a martini one spring evening and mused about the ways of churchgoers. The clear still liquid in the glass looked as though it might have been his tears.

He told about a friend of his, a minister in a prosperous suburb outside Houston. This minister's church, like most churches today, had a lively social club for adult members of the congregation. Often the club held dances and other festivities on Saturday nights at the church house. The minister usually dropped in on such evenings to see how the dance was going, but he never stayed long. He sensed the celebrants would really rather not see him until Sunday morning. One warm night after paying his visit he went back to his study to work on the next day's sermon, then got restless and went outdoors for a walk. Rounding a corner of the church house, he stumbled into a couple petting. A car turned into the church driveway at that moment and bathed the scene in untimely light. The minister recognized the love-makers. They were married but not to each other. Mumbling a polite greeting, the minister hurried on into the darkness.

Next morning after the service he received a visit from the man. "I just wanted you to understand about last night," the man said. "It wasn't anything, really. It was just one of those things. You have a couple of drinks . . . you know?"

The minister knew but saw the situation in a somewhat different light. "It isn't my job to be a talebearer, if that's what you're worried about," he said. "But if you're asking me to condone what you did, I can't. That's something you've got to settle with your own conscience and with God."

The man appeared miffed. "You don't have to be so stuffy about it," he grumbled.

This was the latest of many similar episodes in which the minister had been involved. His patience was at an end. "Look here," he said angrily, "I've let you people turn this church into a social clubhouse and me into a recreation director. But there's one thing you can't take away from me. You've got to let me be against sin!"

His plaintive cry might well be echoed by urban and suburban ministers everywhere. Their churches are being taken over by the weekenders.

Much applause has been heard lately for what is said to be a great revival of religious interest in America. The evidence offered is mostly statistical. Back in 1940 there were somewhat fewer than 60 million members of religious bodies in this country—about 40 per cent of the population. In 1960 there were some 64 million Protestants, 42 million Roman Catholics, 5 million Jews and 3 million of other faiths. They added up to 63 per cent of the population.

Nor did this mean merely that 63 per cent of us listed ourselves casually as having vague ancestral ties to one faith or another. In reporting membership most religious groups count only those who at least sometimes go into a church, if only to fall asleep. What the figures mean is that almost three-fifths of Americans today are actually card-carrying members of specific houses of worship.

It all sounds quite pious. And there are other signs here and there. Posters on trains and buses buttonhole the stubborn nonbeliever and lecture him about what he's missing. "Worship together this week!" he and his family are urged. "The family that prays together stays together!"

There was a time when the sophisticated used to smirk at the "Jesus Saves" signs chalked on the walls and buildings by evangelists. But the bus and train posters are accepted as a manifestation of an important trend in our society. They aren't looked upon as the lonesome cry of what is generally felt to be a rather nutty minority. They are the voice of the majority. The church has graduated from chalked signs to four-color posters, into the very midstream of modern life.

The basic cause of all this new religious fervor, it is agreed, is the parlousness of our time. The world wobbles on the brink of unimaginable catastrophe, it is pointed out. People are turning to God as their last and only hope.

But wait. Presumably if people were worried about nuclear disaster, they would worry as much on Wednesdays as on weekends. This being so the church would be in evidence as an active component of the national life all through the week. If Americans had truly got religion, they would be found meditating before the altar on workweek nights. They would discuss the Scriptures in coffee circles and aboard commuter trains. Businessmen sitting down to lunch would say grace before ordering martinis. There would be a demand for more hours of serious religious discussion on television. Does any of this happen?

In fact, no. Television executives have taken pains to assure the director of the Federal Communications Commission that the American public doesn't want any more hours of serious anything, including religion. If a businessman suggested saying grace at lunch or sought to understand God's will at a sales meeting, he'd be marked as a pale religious nut, probably unfit for further promotion. He'd most likely be eased into some dim corporate backwater where he wouldn't embarrass anybody any more. "See here," they'd tell him, "we're all for religion, and all that, but there's a time and place for everything."

The respected Quaker leader Dr. Elton Trueblood assessed American attitudes toward religion in his book, *The Company of the Committed*. "What we face," he wrote, "is the unexpressed assumption of men and women that the Church of Christ is not in the least connected with what means most to them. The message of the church as understood today is not so much untrue as irrelevant." Religion has nothing to do with the real, the serious business of making a living and running a home. As a Jewish rabbi once put it: "With more and more people, I fear, God is only a weekend hobby."

Religion, honestly practiced, would be a seven-day-a-week affair that seeped into every nook and cranny of one's life. It would have no special time and place but would belong equally at a sales meeting as at a Sunday morning church service. Obviously no such religion is being widely practiced in this country today. There are a few businesses with religious leanings. For example, certain member stores of the Christian Bookstore Association open each workday with prayer. But the very fact that this is worth mentioning indicates how unusual it is.

As the American population grew more mobile in the late 1940's and the 1950's, there was an increasing need for some device by which people could get to know each other as they moved from town to town. Country clubs fill this need for some, but high membership costs scare others away. Other friend-meeting devices have other limitations. Not many towns have community centers, for example. The PTA and other civic service organizations fill the need in some towns but in others may turn out to be disappointing to the sociability seeker. Their meetings may be a little too formal for free socializing and may be dominated by one or two work-oriented members in any case.

But in the churches the lonesome weekenders find a ready-made answer to their yearnings. A church is an organization into which one can step instantly without any preliminary shuffling in the anteroom. The minister, priest or rabbi will welcome you. Catholic and Orthodox Jewish churches will ask that you have or learn their particular traditions, but most other churches won't care who you are or what your religious background, if any, has been. If you express a desire to join a committee or teach Sunday school, the pastor will almost weep with joy. If you like you can participate in the work and sociable functions without ever formally joining the church. The pastor's hope will be that you will absorb the religion by some kind of osmosis and eventually become a full member of his flock. A church offers instant fellowship.

Nor does it cost much. "This place may look like a church," a Protestant minister remarked once in a glum moment, "but what it really is, is a country club with low dues." In fact the individual member is usually allowed to bill himself for his basic dues in almost any amount he likes. Few other sociability clubs dare make this amazing offer.

Like a country club the typical church stands silent and rather bleak from Monday to Friday. Choirs and a few other groups may come in on week nights to rehearse for the weekend. A few women members may drop in to make things for a bazaar. A financial committee may hold a meeting, and perhaps some children's and teen-agers' activities will take place. Some quiet, strictly religious business is conducted. The pastor counsels somebody in trouble and makes arrangements for a baptism. Perhaps he finds time to meditate awhile.

But on Friday night the quiet ends. From then until Sunday vespers the church rocks with activity and seethes with sociable fun. There are dances, picnics, fairs, lunches and dinners. Breakfasts too, for that matter. The children are regaled with parties, games and visits to turkey farms.

At intervals during his busy day the pastor bursts into his study, swallows a cup of coffee, wonders briefly when he'll find time to finish preparing his sermon and rushes out to the next function. The next function is as likely to be a cocktail party as a Sunday school picnic. For the weekenders have taken over not only the church but the pastor as well. They grudgingly allow him to be against sin, but only in the most general terms. They don't expect him to needle them about it or come around with a pious air and spoil their fun. They expect him to be jovially tolerant of their sin symbolizing and perhaps contribute a few naughty witticisms of his own. Most of all they like him to be sociable. Indeed it isn't unusual for a pastor, and his wife if he is married, to be fun or social leaders.

The process of making churchmen just folks began quite a long time ago, of course. Robert and Helen Lynd in *Middletown* noted that the minister of the 1920's was expected to be "a good fellow among the men." But in those days he had a thin tightrope to walk. He was still expected to maintain his pious manner. If he had a beer, he drank it with an ecclesiastical air. He might listen meditatively to naughty jokes and occassionally utter a sepulchral chuckle, but he seldom told such a joke until he was drafted into the Army in the 1940's.

Today the democratization of religion is being completed by the weekenders. Except for his clerical garb, when he wears it, the pastor is often barely distinguishable from his parishioners. The parishioners tend to think of him more as a social director and child guidance expert than anything else. One Protestant clergyman told me about a young housewife who came to him and said she was joining his church on the advice of a psychiatrist. For a moment the minister's spirits soared. Here at last, he thought, was the long-sought marriage between psychiatry and religion. The psychiatrist had become aware of the inner peace that grows from religious involvement.

But it wasn't that way at all. "The doctor thinks I should get involved in activities with other people," the new worshiper said. "What kinds of activities do you have?"

The metamorphosis of church into weekend clubhouse pleases the weekenders. But it horrifies serious-minded churchmen. "The situation is all wrong," says Rev. Clayton Lund, a Congregational minister in Connecticut. "Historically the church has seen itself as being in tension with society, not acquiescent to it. The church is supposed to mold society, not society the church. Its job is to teach and lead whether society likes it or not. In Christ's time, for example, society didn't. Too

many churches are failing to do this job. They've allowed society to tame them. They've been housebroken."

To be housebroken is to take the easy road. A pastor moves into a parish. He wants to make a good record for himself, one that he can show with pride to his superiors in the church hierarchy. The number of souls he saves can't contribute to this record. There is no way of counting them or making juicy statistics out of them. So he throws much of his time and energy into tangible projects that will make good chart material: so many new members signed up, so much money raised, such and such improvements built.

He does this by making his church attractive to prospective new members—by making it what they want it to be. He forms it to fit the needs of the society around it. He sees to it that the church is alive with fun and a-trample with committees, a place in which to meet weekend friends and pursue weekend enjoyments that have little or nothing to do with religion. In the process his basic task, that of saving souls, gets pushed into the background. He makes only token demands on his parishioners in the way of religious observance. He doesn't seriously ask that they change their daily lives or attitudes. He offers them Heaven at half price.

The statistics that come out of all this are bullish and give rise to religious boom talk. The value of new church construction in 1960 was more than a billion dollars. Taken by itself this pleases church leaders. But many of them wonder if it is all an illusion. When a pastor has contributed his energetic bit to the trend, what he has left may not really be a church any more. It may be only a weekend recreation center. His parishioners aren't notably better people than they were before he came. Most are probably the same weekenders they always were—just a little busier. As Peter Berger tartly remarked in *The Noise of Solemn Assemblies*, "The most that can be said is that church members hold the same values as everybody else, but with more emphatic solemnity."

In effect churches have involved themselves in a kind of price-cutting war against other weekend activities. To lure people away from golf, boating and gardening, the churches have tried to make their own type of activity seem inexpensive in terms of moral or spiritual effort. "We've made religion fun," the churchly advertisement goes. "Come and see. We won't ask you to do anything difficult or unpleasant. You can go on with your worldly pursuits and sinful enjoyments. We won't poke our nose into your business. All we really ask is that you join, turn up at Sunday services once in a while and serve on a committee. In return for this minimum effort on your part, we offer a world of gay sociability *plus* a chance at salvation."

Behind this is the hope that religion, exuded from the minister or church walls like some kind of gas, will be absorbed by an occasional parishioner here and there. No doubt it is. And perhaps a billion dollars' worth of church construction is a fair price to pay for the salvation of even a single soul. "At least we get them into the church," the argument goes. "That's the first step. We can't do anything with them until we've done that." But many clergymen grumble that it never goes beyond that first step. Once a pastor has committed his church to the ideal of weekend fun as a recruitment device, it's extremely hard for him to revert to a more serious consideration of religion. He senses too keenly the competition from other churches in town. If he closed down the dance club, he'd lose half his members and maybe his job too.

He knows that newcomers to town, unless they are seriously committed to a specific sect, will often shop for the church that seems to offer the most of their particular brand of fun and sociability. Indeed, there may be a quite clearly understood status ranking of churches in a town. If the town is big enough, there may be three separate rankings, one each for Protestants, Catholics and Jews. The ranking doesn't reflect the various churches' success in producing a climate of deep religious involvement. It reflects the degree to which each has attracted the high-fun crowd or the wealthy. "We're sampling," a newcomer couple once frankly told Rev. Lund. "We're looking for the church where we can meet the most interesting people and the one with the best program for kids."

To attract such newcomers, the pastor must make sure his church gets and keeps a reputation as a haunt of sociable weekenders. And he can never slacken his membership drive, for churches struggle with the same problem that afflicts all organizations in metropolia: old-timers are continually moving away.

Churches flourish as sociability centers somewhat more intensely in the suburban areas of metropolia than in the central city. Sociologist Harlan Paul Douglass in *The Suburban Trend* noted that "City churches have very large fringes of remote and largely anonymous adherents. . . . (But) the suburbs do not easily permit one to be anonymous or irresponsible." An anonymous adherent is somebody who does little but come to the services. He doesn't join the church, serve on committees or attend the picnics. When he leaves church after the Sunday service, he simply goes away. He doesn't stop to talk with the other sociables or get invited to their cocktail parties. He reflects the fact that city people as a rule aren't as anxious to know their neighbors as are suburbanites. City dwellers stay in the city where their Monday to Friday work is and in general draw most of their friends from workweek relationships. Suburbanites live in an entirely different world on weekends. The typical suburban husband's workweek relationships don't often yield weekend companionship. He and his wife must search for it among their neighbors.

Douglass cites figures to show the typical city church has about twice as big an anonymous fringe as the suburban church. At St. Louis Protestant churches, 43 per cent of those attending services in one sampling were people whose names the pastor and the sociables didn't know. At Webster Groves, a moderately wealthy suburb far out from the city, only 23 per cent of the churchgoers were anonymous.

Protestant churches seem particularly likely to be turned into recreation halls. Many Protestant congregations have the power to hire and fire their own ministers. Before hiring a man, they may take him out to dinner to find out whether he is a pleasantly sociable fellow. They are delighted to find he drinks, smokes, plays bridge, had a bet on the last World Series and knows how many cylinders there are in his Volkswagen. Once hired he will find it hard to argue very strongly against his flock's wishes. The church bylaws usually give him a generous amount of power, but this is only on paper. While there are ordinarily certain rules of tenure that protect him from a whimsical or spiteful firing, still few Protestant ministers have long or seriously challenged their congregations' ideas of how a church ought to be run.

Jewish congregations are also autonomous and have power to chart their own destinies. Many Jewish leaders are badly worried about the process of housebreaking. Among them is Rabbi Jerome Malino of Danbury, Connecticut. Dr. Malino is a strong-minded man. He has for many years successfully forbidden card playing in his synagogue. He takes this stand, not because he has anything against the pastime, but because he is keenly aware that a house of worship can become too closely connected in people's minds with ordinary social activity. "Too many synagogues have become community halls," he says.

An article in the *National Jewish Post & Opinion* in 1962 indicated the crisis is already full-blown. "The role of the rabbi has changed to counselor, public relations man, community relations expert and fund raiser. . . . The synagogue emphasis has shifted to that of a social recreation center where Samba lessons are more popular and more prominent than Jewish study groups."

The Catholic situation is somewhat different. Roman Catholic congregations aren't autonomous, nor do they have a voice in choosing their priests. Still a Catholic priest bears responsibility for the morale of his parish. Widespread dissatisfaction will eventually reach the attention of his superiors. Moreover a large part of the priest's job is the missionary one of recruiting new church members. Thus he must make membership look attractive. He must offer to fill some of the weekend fun and sociability needs of the surrounding society.

In this effort he operates under a certain disadvantage. Catholic requirements for religious observance are more strict than those of many Protestant and Jewish groups. But the priest also has a counterbalancing advantage. Historically, and today, the Catholic Church has been considerably more tolerant of alcohol than most other religious sects, and particularly most Protestant groups. Normally the church has no objection to the moderate use of beer at church picnics or liquor at suppers and dances. Most Protestant and many Jewish pastors draw the line at this.

Drinking parties roar around but not in the typical Protestant church house. Members may show up well oiled at the Saturday night dance but must abstain from then on. At about eleven o'clock they begin to invite each other home for nightcaps. By fours and sixes they drift off the church premises, and the dance rapidly shrivels up and dies. Down the street at the Catholic church, meanwhile, the festivities are just now shifting into high gear. Perhaps sometimes out in the lonely night a passing Protestant, on the way home from his own church's faltering festivities, hears the Catholics' undimmed merriment and has a twitch of doubt about his church affiliation.

But the doubt is likely to evaporate the following morning. The Protestant does not commonly feel great guilt about staying home Sunday morning to nurse a hangover. Hangover or not the Catholic attends. The most ghostly silence you will ever hear is that of a large Catholic congregation the morning after a big dance. A pall of headache almost thick enough to see settles over the pews. In the suffering quiet the little bell that rings during the consecration ceremony has the explosive quality of a Chinese gong. For a few seconds after each ringing, if you listen carefully, you can hear the faint rasping noise of the congregation's skull plates settling back into place.

In such ways as this even the rigidly organized Catholic Church is molded, on the local level, to fit the requirements of the weekend society. Of course the degree of molding depends on the individual pastor and congregation, as is true in Protestant and Jewish parishes. But most priests, like most people in general, want to be liked and are sensitive to the soft tides of friendliness or antagonism around them. A young Catholic priest from New Orleans was talking once of the feelings he sensed drifting about his own parish. "My predecessor used to say a short prayer before our Saturday night dances," he said. "But I've abandoned the practice. I have the impression most of our people would rather forget me Saturday night." In a small but significant way this young man was allowing himself and his church to be pushed around by society.

The weekenders are on the whole a warm-hearted and upright folk. The word hypocrisy, which often appears in discussions of church congregations, has been deliberately left out of this chapter. It isn't widely applicable. The kind of smug churchgoing sanctimoniousness that was a favorite target of writers in an earlier age apparently doesn't exist in reportable amounts today. A surprisingly large number of people, buttonholed, will tell you with great honesty exactly why they go to church and what they hope to get out of it.

And any grumbling about churches would be mere dyspepsia if it disregarded the genuine selflessness still represented by these strangely evolving organizations. The weekenders through their churches often display a generosity so great that it brings a tear to the startled eye. They take care of the sick, the hungry and the lonely. They go miles out of their way to carry a word of cheer where it is needed. They play Santa Claus to orphanages. They send their choirs out to hospitals and homes for the aged. They collect money, food and clothing for the destitute. They worry about the ill fortune of others. They do the corny and magnificent things that make men and women walk one inch off the earth like gods.

Yet their churches are becoming less and less like churches in the traditional meaning of the word. Perhaps in some ways this trend is not quite so hurtful as the more alarmed religious leaders would have us believe. The temptation to moralize is great. But I am not quite fool enough to yield.

9. The Nesting Instinct

SOME BIRDS build fancier nests than others. But however fancy it is, the bird usually finishes it. There comes a time when he decides it is adequate and he attempts no further improvements. Weekenders, too, build nests. But the weekender's nest is never finished.

The nest may be a rented apartment in the city, a ranch or split or Cape Cod in the suburbs, a two-room cottage by a lake or a big rambling old house out on the metropolitan fringe. It may be the weekender's year-round home, it may be a summer place or just a weekend place. The weekender may have two such nests or even more if he is wealthy. But no matter how he is fixed for nests, he spends much of his precious weekend time making improvements.

The weekender can't stop working on his nest. It is his haven from the loud, disharmonious workday world. It is the place where, he feels, he can gather and knit whole again the little pieces of his soul that are chipped off each week. But it is more than that. Like all the weekender's other properties it is an expression of what he believes is his real self, the self that gets fragmented and obscured from Monday to Friday. Perhaps it would be more accurate to say his nest expresses what he would like to think is his real self, or what he would like others to think, or both.

167

A housewife of course normally spends much of her work-week in the same house or apartment that may be her weekend nest. But as she is a different woman on weekends, so is it a different dwelling. Her workday self—down-at-heel loafers and random hairstyle—is not the self for which she would like the world to remember her. The prettier and more sparkling self that blossoms Saturday night is the one she is likely to prefer. The home from Monday to Friday is mostly a place of work. Baskets of laundry stand in the hallways. The vacuum cleaner is parked under the kitchen table, and people trip over the cord. The air is heavy with work, flurry and pine oil disinfectant.

But on weekends the home becomes other things. It may become by turns an amusement center, a nightclub and a retreat. It reaches for an atmosphere of good living. The baskets of laundry, the vacuum cleaner and the smell of pine oil are gone. Expensive crystalware appears on the dining room table. The housewife may continue to work, but now it is likely to be a different kind of work. What she did during the week was mainly maintenance—keeping the place running. Now she may spend the better part of a day preparing for a dinner party at which she can show the nest off. Or she may devote much of her time to nest improvement. She plants tulips, repaints the bathroom, refinishes a coffee table or roams antique shops in search of some wobbly piece of furniture that can be propped up in a problem corner of her living room.

For most other weekenders the nest is more starkly set off as a weekend haven. They spend the greater part of their waking lives from Monday to Friday in other people's buildings, designed and decorated according to other people's tastes. This is true even of top executives who have a nominal privilege of decorating their own offices. The *Wall Street Journal* once planned an article on executive suites and sent a young reporter out to gather facts. He interviewed the executive vice-president of a company whose publicity agent had sung loud songs about the way key employees could express their own individualities in their offices. The executive V.P. was amused. "Hell, son," he said, "if this office is my individuality, I belong in a nut house. They sent some interior decorating gal in to help me fix the place up. She had ideas about color keying and all that kind of stuff. When I said I wanted a refrigerator for beer, she thought I was a funny man. Individuality? Haw. What this expresses is the kind of executive the stockholders think I ought to be. It's my image of myself on the cover of *Fortune*."

The weekender's nest gives him a chance to surround himself with what he considers a personally expressive environment. This is why he works on it so long and hard, and this is why he can never finish it. Personality is too complex and subtle a thing to be expressed exactly in the solid materials of which nests are made. The nestmaker has a blurry vision of the mood he wants his nest to create, and he can think of hundreds of improvements which will contribute to the mood. But he has no precise, over-all vision of the way the nest will look when finished. He can only try the improvements one by one, see how they look and proceed to the next. Moreover, his inner moods shift subtly day by day as he is subjected to the constant stream of diverse influences that nobody in metropolia can escape. He visits other people's nests, reads home-and-garden magazines, becomes aware of new design trends, soaks up new approaches toward the ideal of gracious living. His feelings about what the good life must consist of may not be quite the same from one weekend to the next. All this creates a constant slow change in his vague plans for improving his nest.

He begins projects and changes the blueprints in mid-course. He may finish a project, be more or less satisfied with it but twelve months later tear it down in favor of some new idea. One nestmaker, notorious in his circle for being unable to leave well enough alone, spent several weekends pine paneling his dining alcove. He finished the paneling to a high gloss. Then he began to notice the tendency of Howard Johnson restaurants to have glossy paneling. If there is anything a nest shouldn't look like,

it is a Howard Johnson restaurant. So the nestmaker spent another weekend dulling the gloss with steel wool. Not much later
he began to feel the whole idea of natural wood paneling was
becoming common, a thing for the masses. Every new split-level
house had a pine-paneled recreation room. Even Howard Johnson restaurants were starting to move away from solid paneling
and were going in for open-slatted room dividers and large
potted plants. While in this quandry the nestmaker chanced to
visit a gracious old home which had white dadoes and walls of
Wedgewood blue. This struck him as the absolute height of
quiet good taste. So he ripped out his paneling, sawed it down
to make a dado and redecorated the room in blue and white.

This made the furniture look wrong. It was modern and
should have been antique. Moreover the floor was in bad shape
from incessant reconstruction. When last seen, the nestmaker
was poring over furniture catalogs and wondering about the
price of old-fashioned pegged flooring. He believed that when
he had the furniture installed and the floor down, the dining
alcove would at last be as he wanted it. An unlikelier belief was
never believed.

The most notorious nestmakers are suburbanites with their
paint brushes, power saws and grass seed. But city-dwelling
bachelor girls could probably claim the championship for
renovations of the major-upheaval type. The suburbanite commonly potters about his place every weekend, painting something here, digging a flower bed there, constantly busy with an
endless series of usually minor improvements. The single girl
in her apartment may pass several weekends without doing
anything beyond ordinary care and maintenance. But suddenly
a weekend comes when she decides she is sick of her dusty-rose
walls or realizes with a start that the place looks like the reading
room of a library. (A few months ago, embarked on a self-
improvement program, she had striven to create a comfortable
bookish look.)

So with furious energy she spends a weekend turning the nest upside down. She shifts the furniture about, paints one wall dark blue, makes draperies of orange burlap, tacks up a travel poster depicting Paris and decorates the radiator cover with straw-jacketed wine bottles. Now the nest has a sophisticated cosmopolitan air, almost what she wants. But a few

months from now she will meet a man who goes camping, wears untidy tweeds, smokes a pipe and eats apples. Her nest, which she hopes he will visit on weekends, suddenly seems inadequate in expressing the fresh-air component of her personality. The French travel poster does indeed show a Parisian street scene, but somehow even outdoor Paris seems indoors. Outdoor people don't visit Paris, paint walls blue or drink wine, especially out of straw-jacketed bottles. So another weekend renovation is launched.

Almost all bachelor girls in improving their nests give thought to the men who will visit them on weekends. "I had a roommate but we had too many arguments about furniture," said a secretary at the Pentagon in Washington. The girl was pretty and it seemed unlikely her men visitors studied the furniture on Saturday nights. Still the subject was important to her. "My roommate had an armchair with a frilly pink slip-cover. It would have been all right in the bedroom but it didn't belong in the living room. None of the men ever sat in it. A bachelor girl can't afford to make her place too feminine."

All nestmakers are similarly troubled by the need to serve two purposes. The nest must express the occupant's own soul but at the same time be pleasing or impressive to other people. Single girls probably find the dilemma more irritating than most other weekenders. Suburbanites and married urbanites like to make their nests impressive to weekend guests but in doing so they usually have no clear purpose. In a vague way they want to be admired or gain status. The single girl often has a very clear purpose. She wants a husband.

Of course this isn't true of all single girls all the time. There are many who follow the philosophy, forcefully stated by Betty Friedan in *The Feminine Mystique*, that a girl shouldn't pour her energies into the great husband hunt but should build a life that will have value independent of marriage. Yet surveys by *Mademoiselle* and other experts on bachelor girlhood indicate the majority still dream of eventual suburban-style security, what Russell Lynes calls "barbecued bliss." This being so the single girl's weekend nest becomes a thing of great importance. She stands at the door and wonders, "How will this look to him?" Her future may depend on the presence or absence of a large brass ashtray, a copy of the *Saturday Review* on the coffee table or a bug-eyed totem mask on the wall.

The nesting instinct doesn't seem so strong among male bachelors. According to the 1960 Census there were in this country some 2½ million men keeping house alone or with roommates not related to them. There were 5 million women in this category. In part this reflects the fact that the marriage market is rigged in favor of men. There are more single, divorced and widowed women than there are men who will marry them. But it is also true that wifeless men as a breed lean more strongly to lodgings where somebody else does the housekeeping. Perhaps this is partly because men in our society have somewhat more opportunity to express themselves through their work and feel less need for a highly personal weekend environment.

Still there are many bachelors who improve their nests as assiduously as do the girls they date. Most bachelors are anxious to give an impression of overpowering maleness to weekend guests. The nest is likely to include a rack of pipes (probably not smoked since college), framed photographs of basketball teams or other male groups to which the bachelor has belonged, a pewter or earthenware beer mug and pictures of Jazz Age automobiles. If the bachelor wishes to play the role of a thinking man, there are also likely to be large numbers of books, some of which he may have read.

One bachelor I met in Chicago liked dark oak paneling. It reminded him of corporate board rooms, men's clubs and yacht club trophy rooms. He wanted to panel one wall of his apartment but hesitated because oak is costly and, once affixed to the wall, would become his landlord's property under the terms of his lease. One weekend he hit on a solution. He built a collapsible panel of oak-veneer plywood like a huge folding screen, long enough to cover one wall of his nest. He held it against the wall by pushing a heavy table against it. Then he spent most of Sunday evening sitting and admiring it. It gave almost exactly the impression of male-style gracious living he wanted.

At a party several weekends later some of his guests moved the table to clear space for dancing. The paneling stayed delicately balanced until a guest blundered into it. The structure fell forward, folded itself around the terrified guest and bore him wheezing to the floor. "My God," he croaked as they pulled him out, "I thought the building was falling down!"

Married apartment dwellers are similarly frustrated by the need to improve a nest not their own. Still they work on it, though not usually as steadily as the suburban homeowner or with the spasmodic energy of bachelor girls. One of the more intriguing examples of rental nestmaking can be seen around garden apartment developments. On warm Saturdays the residents go outdoors and cultivate little plots of flowers near their doorways.

Children swarm over these plotlets all week. The ground, so carefully spaded and peat-mossed on Saturday, by the following Friday will have returned to its original state of claylike hardness. Only the toughest plants survive, and even these have an air of gloomy despair, as though they really don't care whether they live or not. Fencing in such a plot or marking it off with string doesn't help. In fact it makes matters worse, since all children are bound by a code that requires them to enter an enclosure of any sort. Yet despite the promise of almost certain failure the plotlet cultivators are out there weekend after weekend. No doubt some are working just to be working. Others perhaps are nursing dreams of the gracious suburban homes to which they will one day graduate, gaining a whole quarter acre for children to trample instead of just a plotlet. But most of the plotlet farmers are simply obeying the nesting instinct. Each seeks to make his nest look different from every-body else's. Each wants his nest to express his own personality rather than that of the apartment architect.

Urban weekenders who can afford it (and some who can't) often try to avoid the frustrations of nonownership by buying weekend cottages on lakes or at sea shores, or weekend houses in the rural fringe areas outside metropolia. On Friday night they leave town and hurry out to their weekend nests, and on Sunday night they creep exhausted back to the metropolitan center. In this way the weekend centrifugals believe they gain all the advantages enjoyed by suburbanites but avoid the work-week hell of commuting. It would be reasonable to point out that Friday and Sunday nights are absolutely the worst times to be driving respectively out of and into a metropolitan cen-ter. These two harrowing journeys may exceed in misery a whole week's worth of the routinized commuting logged by the average suburbanite. But no weekend centrifugal will admit this, except perhaps to himself on Sunday night.

The urbanite's shore or country place is the most starkly defined of weekend nests. He may dream of retiring to it some day and spending seven days a week improving it instead of just two. He may spend vacation weeks in it. But most of the year it is the haven to which he flees on weekends. He thinks of it as a place in which he can be at peace, far from the metropolitan crowds. In truth he is likely often to become fretful and bored. Solitude to the average sociable weekender is more pleasant in anticipation than in actuality. Having fled to his country place Friday night, he may flee back to the city Saturday night to attend a party.

Or conversely the metropolitan crowds follow him out to the country. This is particularly likely to happen in business execu-tive circles and in the upper-middle regions of the entertain-ment, broadcasting, publishing and advertising industries. Somebody of high status buys a weekend place in a small rural or almost rural community. On Mondays he brags about it.

He brings back tidbits of earthy wisdom handed him by the farmer who is his neighbor, the old-time handyman who fixed his car for two dollars when metropolitan garagemen had advised him to buy a new distributor, the local mailman who is so funny he ought to be on TV, or the cracker-barrel group at the general store into whose circle the centrifugal believes he has been admitted. In truth these people are probably not as rustic as they like to make themselves seem. They have correctly sized up the centrifugal as a man who has money and can be induced to inject it into the local economy. His bucolic tales however sound enviably nonmetropolitan to his city colleagues. They begin to wonder what it is like out there at Butternut Hill.

In time the centrifugal may invite some of them to spend a weekend with him there. He may show up in the city on Mondays with bags of apples, raspberries, pecans or artichokes from his weekend farm. What his friends won't accept, he gives to his subordinates. The trash cans at bus stops and railroad stations around the city fill up with soggy paper bags leaking raspberry juice. Eventually some of the centrifugal's

friends and subordinates, particularly those with an eye on his job or on jobs close to him, decide to buy property in Butternut Hill too.

It happens everywhere. It happens among Chicago and Cleveland and Milwaukee weekenders who build nests around the Lakes, San Franciscans and Los Angelinos who range along the California coast and east into the desert, St. Louis centrifugals who head into their city's Ozark hinterland, New Yorkers who seek their half-wanted weekend privacy northward in New England. What was once a rural-fringe town becomes almost a weekend suburb, awash with cocktails and sociability as was the city all had thought to escape.

The local natives may grumble that their town is being spoiled, but this is only their public talk. In private, contemplating their bank accounts, most are quite pleased. "They know a good thing when it comes their way," commented a New York advertising-agency chief who bought a weekend place, complete with red barn, in Connecticut. "I decided to take a few days off one week and went up to my place on a Wednesday. It was the first time I'd been there on a weekday except in summer. The rustics weren't expecting any weekend folk, and I caught them with their act down. While I was walking around in the village center buying food, I met the guy who fixed my water pump. I'd never seen him in anything but faded denims and muddy boots. This particular evening he was taking his wife out somewhere, and he was in what might have been a Brooks Brothers suit."

The adman went on to speculate that the whole pastoral community might have been a gigantic act designed to con him and other centrifugals. Perhaps a general store was hastily established with local Chamber of Commerce funds when the first centrifugal moved in. A bright young man was dispatched across the country in search of a cracker barrel. An order went to Sears, Roebuck for a shipment of denim work clothes, and these on arrival were soaked in bleach to fade them. Somebody procured a supply of hay stems for chewing. TV antennae were camouflaged in treetops, Volkswagens were traded in for dented pickup trucks and the mailman was presented with a copy of Captain Billy's Whiz Bang on the understanding that he memorize all the jokes.

Except for his determinedly bucolic frame of mind, the urban centrifugal in his weekend nest behaves exactly like a suburbanite. He spends most of his time in what he calls "fixing the place up," molding it to express his personality and present the kind of self-advertisement he deems appropriate. Perhaps also the fixing up gives him a feeling of rootedness. This is something metropolitan man often lacks during his restless workweek and urbanites particularly may lack in their un-owned apartments. (The suburbanite typically doesn't own his home either. A bank does. Still he is commonly referred to as a homeowner and often kids himself into believing he really is.)

The centrifugal has all the tools of the suburbanite's week-end trade. He has a hammer and saw, a putty knife, a pick and shovel, a wheelbarrow and one of those things that dribble fertilizer on grass. On Monday morning he has all the suburban weekend stigmata. There are abrasions on his knees and scratches on the backs of his hands. The ends of his fingers are red from a scrubbing that has failed to remove paint from the borders of his fingernails. He may also display the peculiar puppetlike walk that comes from stiffness in the lower back.

Yet most centrifugals are anxious not to be thought suburban. Upper-middle urbanites, particularly, consider suburbanism a weakness or blight and don't want to be tainted with it. Perhaps this is one reason why they seldom build or buy a weekend nest that looks like a suburban house or is in anything resembling a suburban development. The ordinary split level or ranch with its neat spare lines and minimum need for wall strength is one of the cheapest and easiest houses to build. But the centrifugal is more likely to choose a complicated modern design requiring a lot of masonry, steel I-beams and glass. Or, if that doesn't suit his taste or bank account, he may seize on a disintegrating farmhouse that was abandoned by its last owner in fear of his life ten years ago.

"They really built houses in those days," he brags to his friends. "Of course there's a lot of fixing up to do, but basically the house is solid." He takes them down to the cellar. "Look at that—eight-by-eight beams. You don't see that kind of thing any more, not in the matchboxes they build today." The guests brush spiders off their clothes and mumble politely.

Unless he really wants work for its own sake, a weekender can break his heart over a place like that. He can put in several years' worth of weekends without making the dramatic sort of improvement he has in mind. One weekend centrifugal I knew bought himself a farmhouse in Vermont. In terms of metropolitan real estate values it was a bargain: a big house and nearly a hundred acres for less than $10,000. I spent a weekend helping him clear out the cellar. It was full of rotting cider barrels and spiders which, if displayed in a zoo, could have been labeled small tarantulas.

My heart wasn't in it. It seemed to me the house needed so much work that my friend could save money in the long run by dynamiting it and starting anew. It was badly out of plumb and needed jacking up. This operation would probably ruin the already warped upper floors. The roof leaked copiously and this over the decades had caused untold damage within the walls. Water was drawn into the house by means of a hand pump that didn't work properly. All this was intriguingly nonmetropolitan to my friend, and he talked for hours about the quaint rustic qualities of his new weekend nest. He had real roots now, he said. But in the end it beat him. A few years later he sold the place, perhaps to another centrifugal.

Suburbanites sometimes buy houses like that, but in general they prefer dwellings that can at least be lived in comfortably while the weekend fixing up is in progress.

Some of the suburbanite's weekend work can be classed as necessary maintenance. He fixes a leaky faucet, for instance, or attends to some trouble in the electrical wiring. Like Saturday shopping, this kind of work gets squeezed forward into the weekend because the workweek allows too little time for it. Other kinds of suburban weekend work could be called almost necessary. If a family has children, it might make sense to build a playroom, for example. But much and perhaps most of the suburban man's and woman's weekend toil is necessary only in emotional terms. In this category the most conspicuous element is gardening.

The number of owner-occupied dwellings in the United States doubled between 1940 and 1960, from 15 million to 33 million. The amount spent on gardening increased nearly fivefold. Sales of flowers, seeds and potted plants rose from $200 million in 1940 to well over $900 million in 1960. Statistics on more recent gardening innovations read something like the Federal budget. According to the Jacobsen Manufacturing Co., major power-equipment maker, Americans now spend about half a billion dollars yearly on power lawnmowers and other garden machinery. They spend another half-billion on garden chemicals and applicators, $225 million on watering equipment and $225 million on hand tools.

Why do weekenders garden? One obvious answer is that they have been sold on the idea of gracious outdoor living. They spend $400 million a year on outdoor furniture, $150 million on outdoor cooking equipment and $20 million on charcoal.

They are attracted by the image of themselves lolling on cool greensward beneath whispering trees, drink in hand. This is good living in the classical manner. It bulks large in the Friday dreams of the typical metropolitan who spends his working life mostly indoors. The outdoors, large and un-hurried, seems to offer a kind of peace such as seldom appears in the frantic workweek with its constant backlog of irritating little problems. The weekender believes some of these problems, or at least the overwhelming sense of their presence, will go away or shrink to pocket size under the vast blue dome of the sky. Perhaps this sometimes happens. But the outdoors has irritations of its own. It is populated by insects, many of which enjoy puncturing human skin. Sometimes it rains. Often it is too hot or too cold to be called gracious.

Like the urban centrifugals, suburbanites are in search of rootedness.

Sociologists Rolf Meyersohn and Robin Jackson of the University of Chicago surveyed weekend gardening and reported their findings in *The Suburban Community,* a panoramic study of suburbanism. They were fascinated by the way mobile people plant long-range perennials like lilac hedges and baby trees. The nestmaker may guess or be almost certain he'll move away in a few years, yet he plants costly garden ornaments that will take five years or longer to achieve a stature worth looking at. In this way he gives himself an illusion of lifelong belonging such as he can't feel during the workweek when his feet never seem to touch the ground. The weekend is the time for putting down roots, the roots whose lack seems to contribute to metropolitan man's loneliness. As the young spruce or lilac roots reach into the earth, the nestmaker feels vicariously a growing sense of firmness. This is my plot of ground, he thinks. Life may blow me hither and yon like a dry leaf, but I will always have this place to come back to on Saturdays—always, always.

Deep in his heart he knows it isn't true. He has little real hope that the house will become an ancestral home from which he will launch his children into the world and which he will one day bequeath to his grandchildren. Next year or the year after his company will transfer him, or he will find a new job elsewhere, or his rising income will permit him to grow greedy for more house and more acreage. He will move to another home in another suburb, and there he will plant another lilac hedge and another two-foot-high spruce tree. And anyway the children won't want the place. They'll want to plant their own roots somewhere.

Of course gardening also has economic and socio-economic causes. An ordinary house can be made to look more than ordinary through clever gardening. Garden magazines and garden-supply merchants are always talking about the enhancement of property values that results from a velvet lawn or an artistically designed geranium bed. This enhancement probably isn't quite as great as the advertisers of lawn seed would have us believe. But it is a motive for gardening.

Neighborhood social pressures influence gardening too. Weekenders in their nests like to be surrounded by an attractive general environment. A weedy, lackluster neighborhood reflects social discredit on all who live there. The neighborhood is the approach to one's own nest, and guests arriving on weekends will begin to assess their host's status before they come within sight of his garden. Thus suburban nestmakers maintain subtle pressures on each other to keep the whole neighborhood looking gracious.

This is particularly true in the newer suburban communities that have blossomed across the country since the late 1940's. Meyersohn and Jackson studied one such town near Chicago. They gave it the code name "Fairlawn." Its homeowners are mainly young adults, predominantly college graduates, well salaried and heading for the upper reaches of the middle class. An older community nearby, code-named "Le Chateau," is populated by older people with generally smaller incomes and less hope of climbing higher. In Fairlawn, the researchers found, 50 per cent of the residents felt required not only to keep their properties looking neat but to plant at least some flowers. In Le Chateau only 34 per cent felt they were expected to go beyond mere neatness.

Neighborhood gardening pressures are not usually harsh, but they can't easily be ignored. One suburbanite told me of a time when a combination of circumstances led him to ignore his backyard. The grass grew a foot tall. At first his neighbors made good-humored remarks, but when they saw he wasn't responding he began to sense a rising tide of uneasiness among them. One Saturday he saw a small group of neighbors standing against a fence and looking at his meadow. They weren't saying anything, just looking. On the following Saturday he became aware that the weekend roar of lawnmowers was louder than usual. He looked out the kitchen window. One of the neighbors was mowing his grass for him.

The fact mustn't be ignored that some nestmakers truly enjoy gardening. They gain esthetic pleasure from the arrangement and cultivation of living things. Yet when Meyersohn and Jackson asked Fairlawn's garden-conscious young adults to list their favorite leisure-time activities, 75 per cent failed to mention gardening.

And even the 25 per cent who did list gardening as a pleasure may often enjoy it less than wholeheartedly. The weekend is too full of other, mainly sociable, activities. A garden project that could be pleasant if performed in a leisurely state of mind becomes a chore under time pressure. This is particularly true of the noncreative or maintenance aspects of gardening. The nestmaker may spend some rewarding hours planning and creating a new flower bed, but in doing so he assigns himself a whole new group of maintenance chores. He won't necessarily be happy a month later when he must weed and edge the bed in a desperate hour before a barbecue party.

What is true of gardening is true of the weekend in general. The major problem is time. The weekender carries in his mind an image of himself living the good life in his nest when it is improved to his satisfaction. But he barely has time to carry out the improvement projects. Seldom does he have time to do the living.

10. The Game of Family Tagalong

ON THE FLOOR of the new $5 million Princeton Club in New York City is a stone slab that bears a curious legend: "Where Women Cease from Troubling and the Wicked Are at Rest." It may be that wicked Princeton men can find rest here, perhaps alongside the Tiger Bar or under a table in the cocktail lounge. But the part about women is only Old Grad nostalgia and hollow bravado.

The day is gone when the Princeton Club could boot F. Scott Fitzgerald out on the sidewalk because he wanted to take Zelda in for a drink. Today the club permits women to trouble anywhere except the Men's Grill. In fact the official prospectus of the new club took pains to contradict the misogynist legend on the slab. "It will be a family club, with particular appeal to our ladies," Princeton alumni were told. "The member's wife can entertain in the Ladies' Cocktail Lounge and Dining Room. . . . Suburbanites and wives can stay overnight after the theater. . . ." The old Princeton Club had an atmosphere of restful gloom, like a pine forest. The new one is full of bright light and bright colors. "Reminds me of a damned automobile showroom," wept one old gentleman, Class of '09.

Yes, the old days are gone for the Princeton Club. Indeed the old days are just about gone for male weekend sanctuaries of any sort. Men's college and downtown clubs, fraternal outfits like the Elks and Kiwanis, and country clubs once devoted to golf and locker rooms and male drinking: all have opened their doors to wives and in many cases to children too. This is the era of the family weekend club.

Partly it's a matter of economics. Men-only clubs have found it increasingly hard to cope with rising costs of food, drink, taxation and metropolitan real estate. By shifting to a family orientation, they increase the use of their facilities and survive. In many cases they can add profitable new facilities. City clubs operate hotels upstairs above the sociability floors. Country clubs now have beauty parlors, teen-agers' Coke bars and coin-operated laundry machines in the basement. The typical country club is not as lively during the week as on the weekend but at least some money comes in between Monday and Friday, especially through the summer.

But money is not the only cause of the shift to family style. To at least an equal extent the shift caters to a need in the weekenders themselves. As a breed they are not strongly drawn to one-sex activities. Perhaps it would be more accurate to say they show few outward signs of being so drawn, which amounts to the same thing as far as club membership is concerned. Male weekenders may sometimes yearn for a stag evening of poker or a womanless expanse of fairway, but other elements draw them just as strongly the other way. Family-style fun is felt to be the most right and most healthy kind. A man feels vaguely guilty leaving his wife and children Saturday morning to play golf. His wife isn't likely to assuage his guilt, for as she quite reasonably points out she would like to have fun too. Nor will she react kindly if he ducks out of a couples' bridge party Saturday night to play pinochle with the boys.

Caught in the backwash of this feeling, one-sex clubs have found it more and more difficult to attract members, especially members who will use the club facilities often enough to allow for a profit. The Princeton Club's history in recent years has been typical. From a peak of about 4,000 its membership sank gradually to a low of 3,200 in the late 1950's. What members it did have used it mainly as a weekday lunch club, a status-at-noon retreat to which one could bring clients, colleagues and others who were important to one's earnings. On weekends it was often deserted and rather ghostly, populated mainly by young bachelors and lone alumni on business trips.

Drastic changes seemed necessary if the Princeton Club wasn't to collapse. In particular something had to be done to increase the use of the club on weekends, to make it more than a workweek restaurant. It was obvious to club officers that men were no longer greatly interested in stag weekends of any sort —or, if they were interested, their wives pointedly weren't. Thus the Princeton Club abandoned old traditions and converted to a family point of view, with appeal to "our ladies." Membership immediately began to rise again. Today it has passed 5,500, far more than the club ever had in its life, and is still climbing. On weekends it rumbles with coed sociable activity which barely obscures the rustle of money changing hands. Solvency and survival seem likely.

The family style of weekend life may have risen to prominence because Saturday and Sunday are the only days when the typical metropolitan family can be together. The husband and father spends his weekdays at work, normally leaving home early in the morning and not returning until supper time or later. Children aged over five spend the bulk of their waking hours from Monday to Friday in school and in the schoolmate society. The mother is home alone or in the society of other mothers. The family is split into three distinctly different patterns of life among three different sets of companions.

This troubles many metropolitan husbands and wives, at least those who are trying conscientiously to make something valuable out of the family unit. It seems rather fruitless to form a family and, in a few years, watch the members divide along separate paths. The feeling is that a home ought to be more than a mess hall or a telephone-equipped headquarters where the members drop in occasionally when their business is concluded. A family ought to have a sense of common destiny, the metropolitans believe, some bond stronger than the mere fact of eating and sleeping in the same house.

The weekend is the time when this bond can most easily be formed. A hundred years ago, when the majority of Americans lived on farms, the knitting together of families was accomplished largely through workday activities. A farmer and his wife toiled on the farm together. They had different duties, but each complemented the other. They were in sight or hailing distance of each other most of the day. The wife knew how the farm was managed and in a pinch could take it over by herself. At an early age the children went to work in the family business. They started with simple farm chores and eventually, when they grew big enough and smart enough, could share all of their parents' work. The farmer typically hoped to achieve retirement, not by means of a pension but by means of sons, whom he trained for the day when he could hand the enterprise over to them.

Today this whole situation is reversed. The ordinary metropolitan family in seeking to establish a sense of common purpose must look to its period of leisure, not work. Work in metropolia doesn't knit families together. If anything, it divides. The father goes off each Monday morning to a company that may be only a name and a vast mystery to his wife and children. He doesn't train his sons to take over his job. Most of their job training is handled by other people, in schools at first and then in company training programs.

The metropolitan wife may not only be unable to understand or share her husband's work ("He's in electronics, but don't ask me what he *does!*"), but she may even resent his doing it. The complaint is often heard in the offices of psychiatrists and marriage counselors. The housewife imagines her husband as living his workdays in a big bright world of clever people and stimulating ideas. Meanwhile she is stuck at home with the kids, her education ended, her intellectual growth at a standstill. Her husband would argue that life at the plant or office isn't all that interesting. Still her point may be reasonable. There may be a real danger that he in his continuing growth will leave her behind.

Thus the weekend becomes the time when the metropolitan family tries to knit together its fragmented self.

One method is to make "family projects" out of ordinary weekend jobs. Man, wife and children together redecorate a playroom. The children are led to believe they can choose the paint colors. In telling about the project later the parents will proudly announce the children did indeed choose the colors. The parents may say also that the children did most of the work. Perhaps the parents really believe this, but it is unlikely to be the strict truth. What usually happens in practice is that the parents exercise the difficult art of vetoing by agreement. "Yes, dear, I think purple would be a lovely color for the window frame, but since we already have orange drapes, don't you think . . ." And as the youngster squishes a paint roller up and down the wall a parent stands quivering behind him, hands tensed as though to catch first the roller and then the child should one or both fall. Finally the parent can stand the strain no longer. He snatches the roller from the small inexpert hand. "Here, let me just touch up a little," says the parent, and paints the rest of the wall himself. But with luck the atmosphere of family cooperation can still be preserved. The child can be sent to get more newspapers for covering the floor or put to work measuring something which the parent will later remeasure himself.

Of course it is easy to be too cynical. Like all currents in our society the idea of family-shared weekend activities is in friction with a strong countercurrent that is equally if not more exaggerated. There is a tendency to heap scorn on all attempts of families to enjoy themselves and grow together. The tendency is most marked among young intellectuals without families of their own. I once saw an essay written by a Vassar senior

and submitted first to a number of literary quarterlies and then to some men's magazines, all of which rejected it. The girl was trying to explain her intention not to marry until she was thirty. "Marriage in itself is all right," she said, "but the trouble is you have to join the PTA and go to family socials." The girl had never been to a PTA meeting or a family social. She was aping a prevailing pattern of thought without bothering with facts. The fact is that family-style fun can be rewarding. Despite what is said of marriage in our society many husbands and wives enjoy each other's company elsewhere than in bed. And the company of children in moderate doses can be absolutely the most refreshing company there is.

But like most other weekender activities the family-fun idea is pushed past the point of enjoyment and into exhaustion. With only two days in which to express family solidarity the weekenders try to express it at every opportunity. A father who snatches an hour's rest instead of going fishing with his son feels a large sense of wrongdoing, though he spent the previous day on a family picnic. And few things make an ordinary mother feel more inadequate than to talk to a childherd, one of those women who every weekend takes Brownie troops out to study old-time butter churns, classify toadstools and watch newspapers being printed. The feeling is that a weekend hour without one's spouse or children or both is a selfish hour.

In fact the feeling has become dogma in many families. Every weekend activity must be shared, whether or not that particular activity appeals to all the family members. As a result many a family outing, instead of being a joyously shared experience, is simply a situation in which some members tag along dutifully with the others. Dad, Mother and children go out together for nine holes of golf. All pretend to be enjoying themselves. In truth Dad is irritated because the kids are slowing the game down. He'd rather be playing alone or with adult male friends. Mother has never taken to the game of golf and barely controls her rage whenever her husband yells, "No, no, keep your *head* down!" The children have a merry time until their parents' irritation begins to be evident around the fifth tee. Dad's ball curves gracefully over the rough and disappears into a dense forbidding forest, never to be seen again by human eye. "Will you stop talking when I'm shooting!" he roars.

The game of family tagalong is played in almost every conceivable area of weekend activity. It has pushed into areas where, ten or fifteen years ago, few would have dreamed of finding it. Outdoorsmanship is an example. Camping, hiking, hunting and fishing were once characteristically male sports. A man left his family behind and spent the weekend in the woods alone or with male friends. They reveled in the roughness of it, smoked pipes, failed to shave and slept in their underwear. On occasion a man might take his son along. His wife might have been irritated at the thought of staying home while he enjoyed himself, but she probably wouldn't have joined him even if invited.

In the late 1940's the rise of the family-fun idea wrought gradual changes in this attitude. Married weekenders began to feel a growing need to demonstrate family cohesion. Women felt it would be advisable to go outdoorsing with their husbands, and husbands felt it would be politic to agree. In the next ten years camping developed from a distinctly minor to just short of a major weekend activity. According to the U.S. Forest Service about 1½ million people visited national preserves in 1950 for purposes of camping. In 1960 camping visitors totaled 6½ million, and much of the increase was accounted for by the presence of women and children.

Family camping represents one of those impossible ideals of the weekenders. Campers seek to escape the workday discomforts of metropolia while preserving the comforts. For most metropolitans the idea of living briefly with nature is enormously appealing. The quiet of the woodlands, the spaciousness of field and sky, the grand self-assurance of things whose only problem is to grow—all this promises refreshment from the jittery life of city and suburb. Yet few families would dare carry the back-to-nature weekend too far. Most campsites have running water and some have hot water, showers and washing machines. Metropolitans making for the wilds are sure to carry other elements of civilization with them, notably gasoline stoves and lanterns, tent warmers, folding cots and ice chests. They share in principle but not in detail Omar Khayyam's dream of woodland simplicity: a loaf of enriched bread, a jug of low-calorie soda pop and Thou beside me, spraying insect repellent in the wilderness.

Men campers are likely to sneer at all this paraphernalia as a mark of softness and blame its presence on the women. Women, in turn, explain it by reference to the children. Actually the children require it far less than do their parents. Youngsters have a faculty of concentration that enables them to ignore heat, cold and mosquito bites when they are doing something they enjoy. They can live a camping experience with a whole heart while Mother broods about the laundry that is piling up and Dad, wrapped coccoonlike in a mass of rope and canvas that is said by its manufacturer to unfold into a split-level tent, nostalgically recalls a day when he camped with bare essentials and a single buddy.

But it is not true, as some disgruntled men have suggested, that the family-fun idea has been advanced mainly by the tagging along of women and children to men's affairs. Men also tag along after their wives. Weekend church activities provide a stark example. Twenty or thirty years ago the preparation of church fairs, bazaars and suppers was almost entirely women's province. The men might perform any heavy manual labor that was required, such as erecting tables, but then they cleared out of the way and pitched horseshoes while the women carried on. Today the men share in almost all the work, even the cooking in some cases. I remember once watching a young husband setting tables for an outdoor supper. He looked up at me mournfully. "My father wouldn't have been caught doing this if his life depended on it," he said.

But probably the most common and determined kind of tagging along is that of parents after their young. When we were kids our parents looked upon our games with amused tolerance and small interest. Occasionally a parent would drop around to watch or perhaps, in a moment of nostalgia, to participate for a few minutes. But most of the time we were left to our own foolish devices. Robert Paul Smith in 1957 described this laissez-faire approach in his book of boyhood memories, *Where Did You Go? Out. What Did You Do? Nothing.* In those days kids were their own games instructors. Older kids taught younger kids how to play mumbly-peg, cops-'n-robbers, ring-a-levio and baseball.

Today through all metropolia the instructors and supervisors are adults. The Athletic Goods Manufacturers Association estimates there are about 3 million boys enrolled in organized baseball today, twice as many as in 1955. (By "organized," of course, is meant established and controlled by adults.) Membership in the Boy and Girl Scouts, also adult controlled, totaled roughly 8½ million in 1960. This was twice the membership of 1950.

Everywhere on weekends you can see parents being pals to their offsprings. Here is a father showing his children how to fly a kite. The kite wobbles into the air, shrugs and wobbles morosely back to earth. "Let me try, Dad," pleads one of the small fry. "Get your hands off it! You're tearing it!" bellows the enraged parent. Here is a harried mother with a den of Brownies in a remote corner of a museum. The architects of museums long ago formed a secret guild, one of whose canons is that rest rooms shall be hidden with care at the end of a long dark corridor in the basement. The mother is saying to one of the Brownies, who is hopping up and down: "All right, dear, if you have to, you have to. Now, the rest of you girls . . ." The mother's voice is full of tolerant understanding but projects an overtone of hysteria.

It is getting harder and harder to find a kid on a weekend

without a parent somewhere in the offing. Model airplane meets, for instance, used to be populated at least 90 per cent by boys. A few fathers came along, and there was a scattering of other men many of whom operated model shops or had same other financial interest in the hobby. Boys built their

models alone in attic, cellar and garage. The only parental contact during hobby hours occurred when their fathers grumbled about the disappearance of razor blades or their mothers complained about the smell of acetone. Today when a lad gets an aircraft model it is likely to become a family project. His father helps him build it, his mother helps him paint it, and his sisters stick on the decals. Then the whole family drives to a field to fly it. There are almost as many taggers along at model meets as there are boys.

Of course there are some fathers and a few mothers and sisters who have a genuine interest in model aircraft. They are delighted to have a boy whose presence gives them an excuse for indulging in the hobby. But most of the adults would much rather be doing something else.

In some cases the boy too would rather be doing something else. A curious kind of circular tagging along occurs, like that of a dog chasing its own tail. The parents believe their son or daughter should do something worthwhile with weekends instead of just loafing around. The parents want their youngster to have some educational or character-building weekend activity. So they urge him or her into the Scouts, perhaps, or into the model-aircraft hobby. Then like conscientious modern parents they grimly enjoy his activity with him.

A hobby-shop proprietor told me about a model airplane meet he once attended at which a high-powered gasoline-engined model went out of control. It howled about the field in crazy looping flight, dived toward a mother who was dutifully engaged in family fun and stabbed her between the shoulder-blades. Luckily she was wearing a thick jacket and wasn't badly hurt. But she was quite annoyed. "This is the last time I come out here," she said. "The *last* time!" But her son couldn't hear her. He was on the other side of the field, playing tag.

Family fun may be an essential ingredient in the complex emotional mixture that makes a sturdy child and helps him grow into a successful adult. Children and teen-agers in metropolia, particularly boys, are likely to need more adult guidance than did those in the self-contained rural communities that once typified America—the communities Robert Paul Smith recalled.

People come and go rapidly through our mobile urban and

suburban neighborhoods. The kids originate from all over the country. They have little or no common base of childhood games and traditions to guide them through a Saturday afternoon, no mumbly-peg to be handed down from big boy to little boy. Moreover they may be up against a shortage of nearby playfield space. The young, weak and timid may seldom get a chance to heft a baseball bat or handle a basketball. Lacking this way of earning success in their young weekend society, they may seek other ways which will get them into trouble. Juvenile delinquency is markedly more prevalent in metropolia than in the true rural communities that still exist. All this requires that adults step in.

But when family fun becomes a duty instead of a joy it goes against the grain of the weekend. Indeed, a weekend of nonstop family fun can have all the treadmill elements of the workweek. Psychiatrist Richard Gordon tells of a patient, a man in his thirties, who was determined to be a model husband and father. He was a salesman and during the workweek labored under heavy pressures from his superiors, his customers and his own ambitions. Instead of achieving a leisurely state of mind on weekends, he simply became involved with a different set of pressures. He tried to be a constant companion to his wife and a never-say-no pal to his children. There were incessant demands on him from family members. Sometimes the demands conflicted. His wife wanted to go visiting. His children reminded him of a promise to go swimmng wth them. He was always makng new promises to atone for old ones not fulfilled. He never had a minute to himself. In the end he developed a duodenal ulcer which nearly killed him.

"Let's use our heads about this," Dr. Gordon counsels patients who get themselves into this kind of trouble. "It isn't necessary for a man and wife to dog each other's footsteps all weekend. Nor does it make good sense for parents to become their children's servants. Family members can share time together, but it would be unreasonable to suppose they wouldn't want to pursue other interests separately."

Man, woman and child do indeed come to the weekend with different ideas of what constitutes a good time. Children have an ability to step clear outside the world of goals and useful purposes and to play aimlessly. They delight in the free and joyous use of their bodies and minds, not caring why they are doing it or where it may lead them. They can splash about in water for hours, so absorbed in nothing that their parents must finally call to their attention the fact that they are blue with cold. This ability to play without a conscious goal is something that seems to atrophy as the individual grows older. The average adult can play with children for an hour or two, and then the game begins to pall.

Men and women differ also in the needs each brings to the weekend. Perhaps the most obvious difference stems from their divergent lives during the workweek and is particularly notable in families with young children. The wife may spend the week with only the children and a few neighbor wives as companions. On the weekend she wants to get out into the world, see and be seen, perhaps use her intellectual powers which she thinks may be shriveling from disuse. Meanwhile her husband may have spent the week in a hurricane of personality frictions. He may arrive home Friday night with the chill statement of one of Sartre's characters in the back of his mind: "Hell is other people."

The feeling doesn't last long. His workweek contacts, based on money rather than love, have failed to assuage loneliness and he will be as anxious as his wife to attend the Saturday night party. But he may not be as anxious to visit relatives Saturday afternoon. He may want to seek an hour of solitude. It may turn to loneliness when he finds it, but he still wants the chance to seek it. In a poll conducted for *Fortune* by the Elmo Roper organization 34 per cent of women counted "visiting" among their favorite weekend activities. Only 23 per cent of men thought visiting was fun. Yet often a husband who subscribes to the family-fun dogma will spend part of his precious weekend gloomily visiting with his wife.

Similarly a wife may tag along to sports events with her husband when she would much rather stay home or go to a garden club meeting. At football and baseball games, automobile races and golf tournaments the crowds are full of determinedly cheerful wives. Some are enjoying themselves. Others are having family fun. Men in our society enjoy watching sports because they can share vicariously in the triumphs of sports heroes. Most women have had a different upbringing. As girls they commonly sought personal success in other media. In the Roper poll 26 per cent of men but only 5 per cent of women listed sports spectatorship as a favorite activity.

Men and women alike seem to enjoy plays and motion pictures, but they differ in the kinds they prefer. When a husband and wife attend a show together Friday night, it is often a case of one spouse gently dragging the other. They would be better off separating and watching what they enjoy with friends of like tastes. According to the Roper poll women tend to dislike dramatic presentations involving crime or horror. Some 42 per cent of women, against 19 per cent of men, named these as unpalatable elements. Women also tend to be bored by Westerns (21 per cent, against 14 per cent of men) and slapstick humor (11 per cent against 4 per cent). Men, in turn, are more often able without regret to stay away from musicals, romances and the drawing-room type of comedy. Such differences in taste are what one would expect in view of men's and women's dissimilar upbringing, life patterns and needs in our culture. But the family-fun dogma sometimes seems to deny that any differences exist at all.

Of course not all married weekenders practice family fun. Some have worked out techniques by which they seem to be practicing it while in fact doing just the opposite. For example, in some upper-middle circles it is standard procedure to take the whole family to the country club for an entire Saturday.

"We were with the kids all day," the parents piously report to friends later. What really happened was that the parents parked the kids at the swimming pool early in the morning and didn't see them for the rest of the day. "I sometimes wonder if I'm supposed to be a lifeguard or a babysitter," grumbled one bronzed young man to a visitor. "Hell, I know I'm being paid to watch kids in the water. But when their folks aren't around, I've got to keep them from throwing ice cream wrappers on the ground and all that kind of thing. I even had to help one kid who couldn't get to the bathroom in time. His folks were out on the golf course. He was eight years old."

Others shun the game of family tagalong openly and also manage to be quite pious about it. The seven-day toiler explains to his children that, although he would love to play with them, he must work this weekend so he'll be able to send them to college. This kind of excuse seldom cuts any ice with the kids, but it helps the compulsive worker believe he's doing the right thing. That he is may be doubted. I remember once suggesting to a boy who turned out for Little League baseball that he get his father to help him practice on weekends. The youngster shook his head rather sadly. "My father doesn't have any weekends," he said. "He has to work every day." It showed. Boys and girls need adults of their sex to pattern themselves after as they grow up. The weekend may be the only chance a metropolitan boy gets to spend any time with his father, and if the chance is denied him he may be in trouble. This particular boy was in trouble. Not only was he inept at handling a ball but there was an indefinable lack in him that the other boys sensed. He wasn't one of them. They needled him sometimes rather cruelly. The existence at some future date of a pile of money for college would be poor consolation for this kind of lonely torment.

The boy's father needn't have spent all weekend with him. A couple of hours on Sunday afternoon could have been enough. But unlike the majority of metropolitans he wasn't willing to give that much. Perhaps he had watched his neighbors playing tagalong and had concluded it was easier just to go on working.

Maybe it was. Tagalong as many weekenders play it is as exhausting as a cross-country race. "The trouble is, people come to the weekend with a heavy sense of obligation to other family members," Dr. Gordon says. "They feel they have neglected each other all week. On the weekend they try to make up for it." He counsels patients to take the burden of family fun out of the weekend. Spend more time with the family on workweek evenings, he urges. Let the kids stay up a little later sometimes, if necessary. Cut out some unnecessary week-night work. "A weekend should be a time of relaxation, not of obligations."

But sometimes he wonders how many people take his advice. Everybody knows a weekend shouldn't be a time of obligations. Yet somehow it almost always is.

11. The Saturday Intelligentsia

EVERY AMATEUR DRAMATIC GROUP in this country includes among its members a man or woman who once had a bit part in a summer stock production and calls everybody "darling." The experience gained in that unforgettable role of Fourth Bystander is usually enough, later in life, to elevate the frustrated Thespian to leadership in weekend footlight clubs. One such lady operated as director a few years ago in a group that periodically gave plays in a high-school auditorium. She was constantly frustrated by the ineptness of the housewives, insurance salesmen, pipefitters' assistants and bank vice-presidents whom she was trying to turn into stage material. "No, no, darling!" she would wail. "Don't just read the part like a shopping list! You've got to *feel* it!"

One actor who tried conscientiously to feel it was a business executive who, because of a peculiarly mournful face, was cast as Hamlet, Prince of Denmark. This is an extremely hard play even for professionals to bring off. The amateur Hamlet had trouble particularly in the scene where he mourned over the exhumed skull of Yorick. Since no human skulls were available, somebody in the prop department had made a rather realistic substitute out of a large rubber ball, to which he had glued cardboard jaws. Weekend after weekend the executive

rehearsed his part, gazing into Yorick's painted eye sockets
until the directress was satisfied he really felt it.

On the night of the first performance he lifted Yorick's
skull and began his discourse with a fine melancholy tone.
"Alas, poor Yorick!" he said. Then the skull slipped from his
nervous fingers. It landed on Horatio's foot. Horatio and
Hamlet both dove at it, but it rebounded past their clawing
fingers and went bouncing across the stage. The jawbone
flapped in a contemplative gum-chewing motion. As the two
actors watched paralyzed, the skull bounded thoughtfully over
the footlights and crashed among the music stands in the
orchestra pit.

For a while there was dead silence in the auditorium. Then
Hamlet, who had been staring down into the orchestra pit
with morose despair, suddenly seemed to arouse himself. He
turned to Horatio, an expression of surprise appearing on his
face.

"Good Lord," he said. "His head was made of rubber!"

Later he pleaded that this was the only thing he could think of to say. "I was *feeling* the part," he said. But the directress could not be consoled. Not long afterward she resigned. "The trouble with amateurs," she was heard to grump, "is that they're so amateurish."

Of course they are. They realize it themselves. People who work at other occupations all week can't be expected to become skilled actors and actresses in the few hours of weekend time they allot to the art. Nor can they easily become skilled musicians, painters, sculptors or photographers.

But they can become proficient enough to enjoy doing it. And they can become identified with artistic effort to a degree great enough to give them the bright self-pleased feeling of being cultured.

The weekend is the time for seeking the feel of culture. It is the time not only for creative cultural activity like acting and painting but also for sometimes baffled but always eager cultural spectatorship. People on weekends go to operas, art galleries and performances of authentic Latvian folk music in which a large throbbing lady pits her vocal cords against a small pale man at the piano. They go to plays by Bertolt Brecht. They watch New Wave movies in which the characters become greatly upset at the sight of knotholes in pieces of wood and mope intensely when a child walks by with a balloon.

The ideal of culturedness is part of the great general weekend ideal, the aura of living the good life. But it also has special causes of its own. In particular the weekenders' urge to be cultured may be a reaction to the cultural vacuum in which they believe they live during the workweek. As metropolitans they spend their workdays in occupations which it is customary to scorn as lacking esthetic or uplift qualities. They are afraid their jobs of housewife, salesman, executive or clerk tend to create one-ply men and women. They doubt that anything connected with the making of money, the conduct of business or the establishment of a home can offer much in the way of culture. All this belongs to America's materialistic surface. Hardly anything else in the twentieth century has received more derision and contempt.

America, the world's richest country, has long felt guilty about its material success. Europeans since Charles Dickens have characterized Americans as a rather gross boorish people who know how to make money but lead otherwise empty lives. Sinclair Lewis in the character of Babbitt portrayed the archetype of the go-getting American whose life is stale, flat and unprofitable. Later he portrayed the equally sorry reverse. Fran Dodsworth was a pseudo-intellectual snob who rejected America as a land populated wholly by Babbitts and made a cult out of Europe. Neither extreme seems admirable, but it is still the Babbitt extreme that most worries the weekenders.

Many of them, too, must be further troubled by a frustration of their creative urges during the workweek. Except among the talent elite, there are not many jobs in the machine-dominated white-collar society that let the individual end his day with the satisfied feeling of having made something new, of having shaped something with his own mind and hands. The need for this feeling seems to be almost universal among men and women. The weekend offers an opportunity to seek it. The weekend in fact is the time when the whole coarse business of making money can be left behind, and people can turn to things esthetic and intellectual.

The weekend painter is typical. General Eisenhower and Winston Churchill are notable examples of this particular search for contentment. On a more ordinary level the weekend painter is as likely to be a woman. She may be launched on her artistic weekend career when somebody gives her a paint-by-numbers kit. These kits are virtually foolproof and usually result in a painting which, while it lacks subtlety or delicacy of feeling, has a quite professional look. Inspired by this, the

new artist next plunges into some efforts of her own.

"I tried to catch the mood of the place," she tells a friend later, displaying a seascape in which the ocean looks something like wrinkled blue celluloid. The friend searches desperately for some penetratingly appreciative remark but can only think of, "Oh, it's very nice."

"Recognize it?" asks the artist. "It's Barnacle Point, where we ate the lobsters that time."

"Oh? Oh, yes. Yes. Very nice." Still rummaging for some more intelligent comment, the friend at last finds one. "You've caught the brooding quality of the place."

The artist's face grows radiant, and the friend realizes with sudden horror that this was too much praise. But it is too late to recant. "Here, you take it," says the artist. "I paint so many that I don't have room for them all myself."

The friend starts to protest, utters a hoarse croak and subsides. There is no kind way to refuse. For years to come the friend will hastily hang the painting on a bedroom wall whenever the artist comes to visit.

Men are more likely to take up photography. Most weekend photography is still of the family-snapshot type, but there is a growing trend toward the use of the camera as a medium of art. One man on the West Coast spent a Sunday afternoon trying to take a picture of his fiancée leaping through the air in a balletlike pose. The effort took place at a beach. He wanted the girl silhouetted against the sky, arms and legs flung gracefully, trailing a long silk scarf. "I wanted to catch *motion*," he told friends later, proudly showing them the results which he had mounted on his apartment wall. Some of the photographs did have an interesting quality of movement. But his friends' favorite picture was one that he had not mounted. It was one of the last he tried that afternoon. The girl by that time was stumbling with fatigue and complaining that she'd leaped more than enough for one day. A second before he clicked the shutter she stepped on something sharp in the sand, unbalancing her as she launched into her leap. The resulting picture shows her shambling through the air with the scarf tangled around her foot, and on her face is a look of bleak discontent.

The most common way of seeking an identification with art, and probably the easiest, is weekend cultural spectatorship. Typical of this kind of quest is the Saturday night visit to a summer Shakespeare Festival. When people invite each other to spend weekends at their shore or country places, often Shakespeare provides the climax of hospitality. "We don't really *do* much at the Point, except loaf," the hosts tell their prospective guests. "I mean, don't expect a big social whirl. Bring your oldest, sloppiest clothes. But one thing we do every year is go to the Shakespeare. We thought maybe. . . ."

The guests are flattered to be assumed cultured enough to enjoy the Bard. So they bring their newest, smartest beach fashions and their cocktail-and-Shakespeare wear. And on Saturday night the party goes to "the Shakespeare." The theater is a converted barn that smells of horses and old paint pots. The cultured audience sits on hard folding chairs which are almost old enough to have been built in Elizabethan times. The air of artistic adventure is heightened by the general awareness that some of the chairs may fold up during the performance. The chairs creak constantly as the patrons writhe in a futile search for comfort, straining to pierce the odd British-like accent that American actors always adopt when playing Shakespeare. Overhead, in the dark recesses of the roof, things cheep and flutter. Maybe they are bats.

Summer Shakespeare Festivals have been proliferating in this country since the early 1950's, arising at least partly to take advantage of the weekenders' wish to feel cultured. Some operate in large cities, but most are in rural fringe or resort areas. Among these, one of the most successful is the Shakespeare Festival at Stratford, Connecticut. A story is told about this theater which illustrates some of the weekenders' feelings about culture.

Patrons of the theater in 1960 were variously intrigued, baffled, annoyed and amused by the stage background against which the plays were performed. Instead of ordinary scenery there was a nonscenery made of odd crinkly-textured shapes. Except for the neutral color these shapes looked exactly like huge potato chips. Seeking to show the esthetic reasoning be-

hind this, the Festival's program booklet explained that it was a "curving, plastic continuum. Essentially, it is a sliced-through invisible dome, suggesting a complete atmospheric surround, with neither beginning nor end. . . ."

One hot Saturday night at intermission time the crowd stood around outdoors discussing this and other matters in subdued voices while two girls sang Elizabethan folk ballads. Suddenly above the thin minor-keyed music a man's voice could be heard protesting loudly.

"I've had all the culture I can take!" he howled. "Used to be, I couldn't understand what I came to see. Now I can't even understand the damned program!"

It was an outbreak of rare honesty, and for a moment the crowd stood in shocked silence. Then everybody began to smile indulgently. This coarse unlettered man would have been better off going to a cowboys-and-Indians movie.

Professional critics, and even nonprofessionals who are confident in their tastes, may often be heard to grumble that a cultural work is uninteresting, or that it is nonsense, or even that it was not sincerely conceived and has money as its motive. But the weekend culture seeker doesn't dare. He tricks himself. Afraid of seeming ignorant or insensitive, he can't trust his own tastes. He lets himself be intimidated into pretending enjoyment when in fact he would rather be doing something else.

He goes to see paintings of tin cans, pieces of bent coathanger wire titled "Revelation" and plays in which two characters sit on a bench for two hours and grump. Every cultural work has its audience, and in each case there are some beholders who feel a hard emotional impact. But there are always others for whom the whole episode is a waste of time, and this is sad because there is so little free time to waste. It would be unreasonable to expect all beholders to be affected in the same ways. Yet this is what the Saturday intelligentsia expect of themselves.

The most extreme members of the intelligentsia carry their quest for an esthetic-intellectual sheen so far that they must be accused of making a cult out of culture. They are related to the Upper Bohemians whom Russell Lynes identified during the early 1950's in *A Surfeit of Honey*. They are middle-class people like the rest of the weekenders, but they want it understood that they hate everything about the middle class and are in it unwillingly, like draftees in the Army. To them, the phrase "middle class" is a term of opprobrium. They feel themselves to be above everything it represents. They vociferously hate Hollywood, television, suburban houses, barbecues, college reunions, Cadillacs, church suppers, Mom's apple pie and wall-to-wall carpeting. They shun anything that is identified with mass, or low, culture.

To show that they are above the common herd, they studiously espouse cultural works that have not yet been caught on to by the masses. When the masses grow interested in a thing, the High Cultists drop it with distaste and contempt and reach for something else. Often, lacking anything new to espouse or afraid that to embrace the new all the time may look like faddism, they reach back behind the middle masses and revive something that the middle masses themselves have left behind, like folk music. Or jazz. Jazz was mass culture in the 1920's. It faded in the next decade. Late in the 1940's the High Cultists rediscovered it, turned it into a cozy little cult and discussed it in solemn tones in espresso houses. Then the masses began to take an interest in it, the High Cultists dropped it and the cycle was complete.

The Twist is another example. It became popular in the late 1950's among teen-agers, who are commonly agreed to represent mass culture at its massest. The middle mass of weekenders scorned to dance the Twist in those early years. But High Cultists, ever reaching for some new means of proving themselves, began to Twist about a year after the youngsters did. Relatives of the President soon followed. By the early

1960's the weird pelvic movements of the dance could be seen at any country club or church dance. The High Cultists dropped it like a dead fish.

The High Cultists illustrate starkly how difficult a path the weekender must follow when he chooses to seek the label, "cultured." It is not a quest that leads to relaxation. I watched a High Cultist at a gathering in 1961, during the transition period when the masses were beginning to grow interested in the Twist. Members of the gathering started to teach the dance to each other. The High Cultist sat and sweated in his chair, obviously wrestling with a terrible dilemma. He wasn't sure whether the Twist was still "high" or had become "mass." Several times he got up from his chair, seemed about to join the fun, hovered around the room uncertainly and sat down again. When somebody tried to urge him into the dance, he uttered a mirthless laugh. Then he began to think perhaps it was middle class *not* to Twist. He stood up again, nervously sipped his drink, tentatively waved one leg as though practicing and finally walked toward the dancers with a resolute air. But by this time they had all decided they liked other dances better.

Whether it is a genuine pursuit of culture or just a pursuit of the label, the statistics dealing with it are startling. The statistics have prompted some enthusiastic observers to talk of a culural renaissance in this country. The Economic Research Department of the Chase Manhattan Bank, interested in the effects of social trends on business, has charted the renaissance from its early stirrings in the 1940's. Statistically, at least, we are indeed becoming a nation with a great interest in music, art, drama and literature.

Americans in 1960 spent two and a half times as much on books as in 1946, the Chase reports. They spent twice as much on theater and opera tickets. The apparent cultural growth has been particularly accelerated since 1955. In the half-decade 1955–1960, spending on books rose 65 per cent, and on theater and opera tickets 49 per cent. This country, the Chase points out, now supports more than half the world's professional symphony orchestras. The people who visit New York's Metropolitan Museum of Art on a single Sunday would twice fill the giant Madison Square Garden sports arena. The museum's annual report in 1962 stated that attendance had more than doubled from 1955 to 1961, from under 2 million to 4 million.

There are undoubtedly many reasons behind such figures as these. Rising educational levels and rising incomes must certainly have contributed to a growing awareness of culture and a capacity to take advantage of it. And perhaps a cultural renaissance of some sort actually is taking place.

High Cultists are no doubt the most energetic contributors to the statistics. But most of us harbor streaks of high cultism which rise to the surface on weekends. It is unfortunate that this is so. If we spent less time doggedly appreciating what we think we ought to appreciate, and more time simply liking what we like, we'd reap a few more enjoyable weekend hours. We might even become cultured without trying.

The weekender's nervous cultural quest even sours his enjoyment of the more modest creative offerings that may engage his attention over the weekend. Not only High Cultists but most weekenders feel it is chic to speak unkindly of big-budget movies featuring Elizabeth Taylor and the population of Rome, Hit Parade music, magazine stories in which the heroine discovers love is more important than money, TV whitecoaters in which the doctor decides his patient's gall bladder is worth more than the hospital rules and historical novels in which the author deems sex and mayhem to be worth more than history. People absorb this kind of material comfortably on workweek nights. They know it isn't "high," but they can think of it as a device for relaxation. They feel they are entitled to let their minds droop after a hard day's work. On Saturdays people feel uncomfortable with the same material. They feel they should idle in a less idle kind of way.

A college-educated housewife admitted once that she watched a soap opera on workdays. "I think it's well written and well acted," she said. "But I know it isn't the kind of thing anyone with a college degree is supposed to enjoy. Anyway I'm glad they don't run soap operas on weekends. I wouldn't feel right, watching it on Saturday and Sunday."

Another weekender recalled a Saturday evening when he arrived at a friend's home for a dinner party. As he parked his car he distinctly saw the bluish shine of a live television screen through a window. But when he rang the doorbell his host greeted him with a book in hand. The TV set had been turned off. A hi-fi set had been turned on and was playing a Beethoven string quartet.

Undoubtedly many weekend hours that could be quietly pleasant are spoiled by the faint feelings of shame that often arise when we contemplate anything "mass." Cultural leaders often refer to this kind of material as *kitsch,* a German word meaning, in this usage, rubbish. They have a number of quarrels with it. They point out that it doesn't make the beholder think very hard. It tells him what his reactions ought to be, as in the case of an FBI movie where he knows he must hate the gangsters. It has been called "predigested" art. Its effect is to divert modern man from his complicated and often painful reality in such a way that, when he returns to reality, he is not much better equipped to cope with it. *Kitsch* is accused of giving him no new insights into himself, other people or human life in general.

But the question is, how much does the weekend have to do with the reality of the workday world? To a large extent and for many people the weekend is a period of fantasy. It is a time for playing roles and dreaming dreams which the working world has frustrated. It is the time for going to far places in a wistful attempt to leave the world behind. It is the time for dream shopping among the Sunday newspaper ads and idly pondering the high-salaried employment offers.

Mass-audience entertainment with its simple motivations and direct action fits neatly into this fantasy world. Metropolitan man spends his workweek in a huge complex world against which he often feels powerless and in which, after striking out futilely for a long while, he sometimes comes up against the awful fact that one of his enemies is himself. It is refreshing on weekends to retire briefly to the simple world of the televised cop or private eye. Here is a man who is utterly sure of himself. He never wakes up at night and thinks, "When he said this, why didn't I say *that?*" He can always think of the thing to do at the precise moment when it is needed. Small irritations do not beset him. His shoelace never comes untied when he is chasing a crook. He never spills gravy on his suit. When he types his reports, he never gets the carbon paper in back to front. He is not required to question his own motives, and as each episode ends he is in complete control of his destiny.

It is refreshing, too, to read a love story in which everything comes out all right. It is a cathartic emotional experience to identify with a prairie marshal who singlehanded, by direct action, smashes the forces that have risen against him. All this is compatible with the dreams people have on weekends.

But as the viewer sits before his TV set on Sunday night, he hears the aggrieved voices of cultural leaders: "Tch, Tch! *Kitsch!*" The creators of mass material themselves add to their audience's discomfort. Every other issue of *TV Guide* contains an interview with a popular actor who professes to be unhappy in his prairie, hospital or precinct-house roles and wants to do what he calls "serious" acting. It is not a new phenomenon, of course, to find entertainers thinking of themselves as artists, but it does seem odd to find them publicly knocking the medium that pays their salaries. Similarly TV scriptwriters all want to do serious writing and directors want to do serious directing. The presidents of TV networks have even assured the Federal Communications Commission that they would like to do some serious presiding, if only they didn't have their stockholders to think about. They don't believe Ibsen would sell deodorants well enough.

All this diminishes what simple pleasure the weekender might find in mass-produced fantasy. The trouble with his whole approach to culture (as to many other weekend activities) is that he pays too much attention to what other people think he ought to do. We like to think of the weekend as a time when we slip out of the constraints that have held us all week. Actually what we often do is accept a whole new set of constraints. And in that sense it really isn't free time at all.

12. The Ideal of Free Time

CHILDREN HOLD IT to be axiomatic that if a lollipop is good, a bigger lollipop is better. It doesn't occur to them that they might not be able to finish the bigger one or that it may make them sick. Adults have learned through experience that these possibilities exist. But the childhood axiom doesn't fade entirely from adult modes of thought. In areas where adults lack experience on which to base judgment, they often assume that if a thing makes them happy, more of it will make them happier. Or they assume that if a thing is not quite good, more of it will make it better.

Thus do we think about weekends. Some time in the future we may receive the gift of a three-day weekend, or perhaps even one equal in length to the workweek. Industrialists and labor leaders talk of this likelihood as though the expansion of workless time will be an absolutely unqualified blessing. We assume it too. If the two-day weekend is too full of too many obligations or is otherwise not what we dream of each Friday, an extra day will make everything come out all right.

But we may only be looking at lollipops again. Few of us have had experience with three-day weekends except as occasional treats—Labor Day, for instance. What would it be like if such a big lump of workless time came regularly? Would we

221

know what to do with it? Would we come any closer than we are today to the ideal of the good life?

One way to probe these questions is to consult some people who have actually lived through the experience of a regularly scheduled three-day weekend. Such a group existed a few years ago on the West Coast. A California aircraft company conceived an idea for a new kind of weekend arrangement. The idea was to take the available workless days and shuffle them about so that some weekends came out longer than others. The management put the idea to the employees. The employees liked it and voted to try it.

The "new calendar," so called, worked in units of four weeks. Each unit contained two ordinary two-day weekends, a three-day weekend (Monday being the extra day) and a single day (Sunday). It started in January, 1958. Sociologist Rolf Meyersohn, then attached to the University of Chicago's Center for the Study of Leisure, became interested in the program and resolved to keep an eye on the new calendar to see how well it worked. His first probe indicated everything seemed to be in fine shape. After a month's trial almost half the employees liked the new calendar "very much," another 29 per cent liked it "on the whole" and only 14 per cent didn't like it. The rest didn't care one way or the other.

Half a year later, in July, Dr. Meyersohn looked over the situation again. It was logical to suppose people would like the new calendar even more in summer months when the kids were out of school and the long weekend could be used for far trips. But instead of enthusiasm Dr. Meyersohn found mounting annoyance. In July only a fourth of the weekenders liked the idea "very much," 29 per cent still liked it "on the whole" and 32 per cent were ready to scrap it.

Four months later the percentages had changed still more. The employees voted two-to-one to abandon the new calendar.

What was the trouble? The most common complaint was about the one-day weekend. Employees couldn't get used to having just one day off between periods of work. This would argue that they welcomed their free time and perhaps found the good life in it. But a curious twist of reasoning was involved here. The one-day weekend was the one in which employees repaid a day (Saturday) borrowed to make a prior three-day weekend. Dr. Meyersohn found among them a distinct feeling that they were repaying this day for "services not rendered." The third day of the long weekend turned out not to be valuable to them. They didn't feel they were getting enough use out of it. They felt they were repaying a good Saturday for a so-so Monday.

Employees and their families didn't know what to do with the third day. In January when the new calendar started, half of them had plans for using the long weekend. By July only a third had any plans. As the new calendar rolled through its eleven-month life, the long weekenders used the extra Monday more and more for household chores.

This experience offers small hope that a three-day weekend would be a great deal sweeter than what we now have. If the magic aura of good living eludes people today, the evidence doesn't show that their problems can be solved automatically by lengthening the span of their workless time. The problems have their roots elsewhere.

A few of the problems might be alleviated a little by an extra weekend day. The copious leaking of work into weekend time might be less bothersome, for instance. There would be more time to absorb the work. But other problems might only be made worse. For example, in a work-worshiping industrial society, leisure has always been considered a frothy dessert to be served after a good square meal of work. Already there are many people who find it hard to get through a weekend without a clear strong purpose, and most of us at least sometimes feel lost and adrift by Sunday noon. In this state of mind what of value could we find in a workless Monday?

Other problems might not be affected one way or the other

by an increased weekend span. The compulsion toward visible
fun would probably keep people hopping in a three- as in a
two-day weekend. They would still be tense with the need to
be likeable. There would still be the strong emotional requirement that they improve their nests. The obligations of
family tagalong and culture would still rest heavy on their
shoulders. Sin and its symbol would arise, evidence of people's
great need to feel free. But there might not be much more
really free time time on the longer weekend than on the
weekend we know today.

If you wish to see the most stark kind of human evidence
that weekends can let people down, you need only spend a
Saturday or Sunday hanging around a hospital emergency desk.
Take Norwalk Hospital in Norwalk, Connecticut. This is a
moderately large hospital that serves not only the prosperous
manufacturing and trading city in which it is located but also
a vast surrounding area of suburbs populated by New York
City commuters and their families.

Saturday, January 6, 1962, was an ordinary winter Saturday.
The weather was clear and cold in that part of the country.
There was skating, sleigh riding, and ice on the sidewalks.
Home handymen and other nestmakers worked indoors rather
than out. There was little pleasure in driving, nevertheless
there was much driving from one place to another and much
drinking to get warm. As the day dawned, doctors at Norwalk
Hospital knew they'd see the results of falls on ice and off
sleds, home carpentry mishaps and too much alcohol. They
were right. During the day sixteen adults and two children
came in the emergency door to be patched up after severe
nonautomobile accidents. This was twice as many as there had
been on any day during the previous week.

There was nothing in this of course to indicate people hadn't
been enjoying the weekend. But as other emergency patients
came in, mostly toward evening and at night, the pattern of

the day grew clearer. Four women and four men stumbled or were carried in complaining of severe abdominal pain—perhaps overeating, perhaps ulcers, perhaps simple tension. Eight of them: also double the number of any previous weekday. Three people arrived clutching at their skulls, begging relief from intolerable headaches. A man was led in shivering and hallucinating, in the throes of an alcoholic seizure. One man and one woman needed treatment for injuries sustained in fights. Two women arrived weeping. Their trouble was diagnosed as anxiety or hysteria. One man and one woman were brought in by the police, and on their admittance forms went the laconic and curious notation: "Found wandering street in dazed condition."

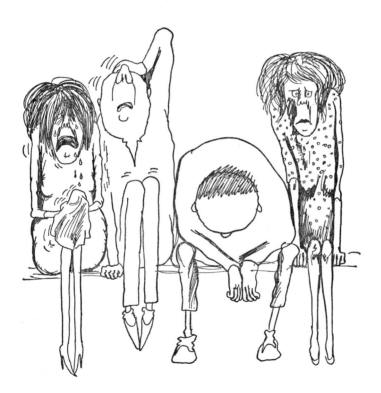

"Saturday night," said an intern, "that's when we really earn our pay."

Evidently the weekend for many people is not what it could be or should be.

Why isn't it? There is no shortage of opinions. All kinds of people stand ready to tell the weekender what he ought to do. He ought to improve his mind. He shouldn't watch television so much. He ought to relax. He should become physically fit. He should seek solitude. He should spend time with his family. He should go to church. He should throw his inhibitions away and whoop it up.

The weekender keeps hoping he'll find a formula that works, and he listens anxiously to all the opinions. He worries about the views of recreation directors, Marine Corps officers, Presidents, visiting Italian novelists, young writers just back from Paris, old writers living in Spain, farmers from Iowa, intellectuals from New York and weathered old ladies who make maple sugar in Vermont. The country swarms with people who claim to have some special wisdom about the way free time ought to be used.

The weekender lets himself be pushed around. When he would rather be fishing he goes to an art museum and looks at paintings of people with both eyes on one side of their heads. Somebody has told him he should get cultured. At the same time another weekender who would rather be in the art museum is quivering with terror on a pair of water skis because somebody says he ought to get some outdoor fun. As Russell Lynes once wrote in *Mademoiselle* of young women who try to be everything others think they should be: "Theirs is a life that has to be lived furiously in order to get everything in, and yet the essential quality is that of seeming relaxed. . . . While they are reading they will be worried about not being on the tennis court, and while they are indulging their own predilections they will be looking over their shoulders to

see whether their tastes manage at the same time to be personal and yet uneccentric."

The basic assumption behind all this is seldom questioned, that is, that one man can sensibly tell another what to do after work.

The question of what people ought to do when no longer required to struggle for survival has perplexed humankind for thousands of years. But of all the answers that have been given, only one has had lasting value or universal application. It seems to have been developed first by the ancient Greeks. The one thing above all that men and women should find in workless time is freedom.

It was an ideal that the Greeks struggled to make real, followed by the Romans, followed by millions of other people down through history. It was always a struggle against tall odds. The ancients were sadly aware, as we are, that freedom is hard to come by, particularly in urban (and today suburban) life. Such a life is full of entanglements and obligations. The individual may be free in an official sense. He may have the right to say who will govern him, and he may have the protection of law against bullying by those in power. Still he is pushed and pulled all his life by the overwhelming complications of living with other people and making his way among them toward his goals. He always has a hundred things to do at once. Life lies on top of him like a huge octopus. The weight of it doesn't lift automatically when he stops work.

Apparently it was always this way. Epictetus the Stoic spent his young manhood as a slave in Rome. Later he was freed but he knew there is more than one kind of slavery. In his discourse *Of Freedom* he told a story, perhaps partly autobiographical, of a freed slave who strives to make a place for himself in the urban society. He enters the nimble-toed dance that is familiar today in San Francisco, New York, London, Tokyo and every other metropolis. He curries favor here, patches up a grievance there, worries about an opinion here, sidesteps a complication there. "Now, miserable wretch," he howls, "what do I suffer, in being a slave to many instead of one!" Then he begins to believe he'll escape this new kind of slavery if he can work his way up the status ladder and become an equestrian, head held high, above all these petty irritations. But when he reaches that status, he finds the pressures of life are twice as heavy. He keeps climbing and finally becomes a senator. Says Epictetus: "It is then that he undergoes his finest and most splendid slavery."

Epictetus sought his own freedom in the manner of the Stoics. Their way was essentially to cultivate a tough outer hide that would absorb the world's needling, meanwhile preserving a tranquil, free and private self within. A man in the ideal state of Stoicism would have perpetual free time. The outer man might be subjected to all sorts of indignities and annoyances. But the inner man would be free to roam as he chose, calm and content. This was a most difficult philosophy to turn into actual practice, though there were perhaps some who could do it. There may be some who can do it today.

Other philosophers tried other approaches to the problem of freedom. Epicurus thought it was possible to tread one's way through life prudently, doing what work one had to and in time off choosing only those pleasures that didn't bring with them a tangle of irritations and obligations. The Epicureans probably wouldn't have motored to distant beaches or ski resorts, joined church social clubs, taken children to visit historic sites or pulled a single clump of crabgrass from the earth.

Others tried to step sideways out of the ancient rat race. Diogenes believed the happiest man was he who had the fewest material wants. He sought to be as free as possible of both work and workless-time entanglements. He wanted to be independent of all other people, his daily course dictated only by his own far-ranging mind. The story that he lived in a barrel may be apocryphal, but if it is true it shows how highly he valued freedom. Socrates also trained himself to want little, walking about Athens in bare feet and ragged clothes. If these men were alive today, they would not be willing to work in order to buy a boat, a pair of skis or a tennis racket. Nor would they be likely to accept such pieces of leisure equipment as gifts. They would reject anything that might tend to clutter up their lives. A boat would require maintenance. A pair of skis would require long journeys. A tennis racket would require the payment of court fees or club dues. And the acceptance of such a gift would create an obligation to another person. One of the other Diogenes legends is that Alexander the Great approached him in his barrel one day and offered him a gift. Diogenes is reported to have said he wanted only one thing. Would Alexander please move over a little? He was standing in Diogenes' sunshine.

Plato approached the problem in a different way. He was fascinated with the idea of securing freedom (though only for a few) through legislation. He envisioned an ideal state in which a group of free scholars could pursue philosophy, science and the arts in an atmosphere of leisure. Each could ramble along paths of his choosing, not required to drive toward any particular goal, not required to submit reports or produce any concrete results. Plato himself in his lifetime seems to have approached this ideal of a tranquil, contemplative, goal-free leisure. His pupil Aristotle approached it too. Scholars ever since have been enraptured by the idea, and some have gone so far as to call it the only true leisure there ever was. But this seems to be sharpening the definition of leisure to too fine a point. Leisure is tranquil, free of goals and free of pressures, but there is no reason why it must be mainly contemplative in nature. Contemplative leisure is only one kind. Plato himself in his youth was a man of vigorous physical action, a fine athlete as a matter of fact. The name by which we know him is probably a nickname referring to his broad shoulders. He reveled in the free and joyous use of his body. Later he turned to the free and joyous use of his mind.

Today on weekends the search for freedom goes on. As the ancients had to we must face the fact that there are some things we can hardly be free of. On weekends as on workdays we must attend to the body's demands for food, warmth and sleep, and we must take care of our children until they can take care of themselves.

Some of the incursions of work into the weekend can probably be repulsed. Often a society works out ways of handling things that are irritating it. The huge unwieldy metropolia we live in today may in time slowly come apart and resettle itself, allowing more people to live near their places of work.

But the weekender's major move toward freedom, if it occurs, must take place within himself. Whether this will happen, and if so how, are monumental questions. There is simply no basis on which to make sensible predictions. Our society has changed enormously in the past twenty years and is likely to change as much in the next twenty. In forty years it may be barely recognizable. Looking ahead from this point in the 1960's, we can't possibly tell what people in 1980 or 2000 will do in their workless time, how they will feel about it, whether they will be satisfied with it. Indeed we can't even be sure what form that workless time will take. Maybe there will be a three-day weekend. Maybe people will decide it makes more sense to have one day off every two days, or a six-day weekend at the end of every two weeks. We don't know what new kinds of leisure may arise, what new games and gadgets will be invented, what new ingredients may be mixed into the national concept of the good life.

We can't predict but we can dream. Dream of a weekend society in which the work ethic is only a historical curiosity. People don't feel compelled to be doing anything useful. They need no hard tangible goals. They left goals behind when they left work at the weekend's beginning. They are opened up to the world. They are in a state of being receptive to the blue of the sky, the sound of music, the love of other people. They are capable at times of playing as children play, or gazing at a building and wondering why it was made thus instead of thus, or just standing about with their hands in their pockets, thinking of this and that. They don't grumble at the teen-agers who loaf around the corner drugstore. They have nothing against loafing, not on weekends.

And dream of this. These people feel only a minimum of compulsions to do what they don't want to do. The basic requirements of survival are in force, as are of course the everyday laws that keep people from stepping on each other's toes. Only a few other elements exist to constrict these people's freedom. Some are having family fun, but they will stop soon after it becomes tiresome. For most perhaps it seldom grows tiresome, for they haven't been in the habit of doing it all weekend and approach it as a refreshing change. In any case, possibly a resettling of metropolia has resulted in families being together more often during the workweek, and no special burden of obligation rests on the weekend. People are with their families mainly because they feel like it.

There is no compulsion among these weekenders to go out and have fun. Some are having fun because they happen to feel like it at the moment. Some are even working because they feel like it. Nobody is listening to anybody else saying he ought to be more cultured.

This is a beautiful dream. And since it is a dream it can be touched with madness. One day's madness, though, may turn out to be the next day's cold scientific fact. Who knows, perhaps the metropolitan society will evolve a way to handle its painful problems about human love. People in this imaginary weekend society feel free to have the friends they want and not to have friends they don't want. They go to church and listen to the church's ideas more intently than to the chatter of other sociables. When they don't want to hear church ideas, they don't go to church. They improve their nests to please their senses of order and beauty, not to prove things about themselves to others.

Here are tranquil happy people, freely pursuing contentment each in his own way. Here is the good life indeed. Can it really happen?

Well, perhaps not. Perhaps this is too much dreaming. The perfect weekend would be like Heaven and there is probably no such thing available on earth. But there may be a close approximation. We may yet find it.

So hang up the bright ribbons and try again. And think of this. Weekends are like roses. Some are more beautiful than others. But they are all roses.

Acknowledgments

MOST OF THE SOURCES of information and opinion on which this book is based are identified in the text. Those which are not fully identified are listed here.

CHAPTER I: The quotation on well-roundedness is from "What Has Succeeded Success?" by Russell Lynes. Reprinted from *Mademoiselle*; © Street and Smith Publications Inc., September, 1954.

CHAPTER II: The statistics derived from *A Nationwide Survey of Living Habits* are published here with the permission of J. A. Ward, Inc., and the Mutual Broadcasting System.

CHAPTER III: The case story of a love affair between an engineer and his secretary appeared in abbreviated form in "When to Worry About an Office Romance," by Max Gunther, *Good Housekeeping*, March, 1961. It is retold here with the magazine's permission.

The Roper Poll statistics in this and succeeding chapters are used here with the permission of Elmo Roper & Associates.

CHAPTER IV: The remark by David Boroff about the Catskills resort area appeared in *Harper's*, July, 1958.

Statistics dealing with boats and motors were provided by the Outboard Boating Club of America and the Outboard Industry Associations.

The statement dealing with families' ranges of weekend

activities is from "A Survey of 504 Families to Determine the Relationship between Certain Factors and the Nature of the Family Recreation Program," by James A. Wylie, *Research Quarterly of the American Association for Health, Physical Education & Recreation,* May, 1953.

The statistics on spectatorship are from "The Use of Leisure and Its Relation to Levels of Occupational Prestige," by Alfred C. Clarke, *American Sociological Review,* June, 1956.

The figures on sports injuries are from the U.S. Public Health Service's National Health Survey for the years July, 1959, through June, 1961, and the National Safety Council's publication *Accident Facts 1962.*

Chapter V: Data on bowling are from the American Bowling Congress; on clubs and fraternal organizations, from the U.S. Dept. of Commerce; on hunting and fishing, from the Fish and Wildlife Service of the U.S. Dept. of the Interior.

The data on solitary craftsmanlike activities are taken from Alfred C. Clarke's study of leisure and occupational prestige, cited above.

The figures dealing with *Vogue*'s readers and their habits are taken from statistics compiled by the magazine's advertising and research departments.

The discussion of sociability at Park Forest is based on the series of articles, "The Transients," by William H. Whyte, Jr., *Fortune,* June–August, 1953.

Statistics on "neighboring" are from "Contrasts in Neighboring," by Sylvia Fleis Fava; a chapter in the anthology, *The Suburban Community,* edited by William Dobriner, New York, G. P. Putnam's Sons, 1958.

Chapter VI: For the general background of information on which this chapter is based, I am particulary indebted to Dr. John Dydo of the Licensed Beverage Industries, Inc.; and to the series of statistical pamphlets, *True's Entertainment Survey,* published by the research department of *True* Magazine.

The data on weekend drinking habits of alcoholics are from

"Phases in the Drinking History of Alcoholics," by E. M. Jellinek, *Quarterly Journal of Studies on Alcohol,* June, 1946.

The discussion of drinking parties draws on "Sociability, Permissiveness and Equality," by David Riesman, Robert J. Potter and Jeanne Watson, *Psychiatry: Journal for the Study of Inter-personal Processes,* November, 1960; and on "The Vanishing Host," by the same three authors, *Human Organization,* Spring, 1960.

The discussion of "overshooting" draws on *Social Drinking,* by Giorgio Lolli, M.D., New York, World Publishing Co., 1960.

The statistical data on people's actions in small groups are from "Sociometric Status Patterns and Characteristics of Interaction," by Edgar F. Borgatta and Robert F. Bales, *Journal of Social Psychology,* June, 1956.

CHAPTER VII: Statistics dealing with crimes of passion were provided by, and are published here with permission from, Col. Stanley R. Schrotel, Police Chief, City of Cincinnati, and W. H. Parker, Chief of Police, City of Los Angeles.

CHAPTER VIII: For the general background of this chapter I am deeply indebted to Rev. Clayton Lund, First Congregational Church, Ridgefield, Connecticut.

Statistics on church membership are taken from the *Yearbook of American Churches,* National Council of the Churches of Christ in the United States.

CHAPTER IX: Data on consumer purchases of gardening and outdoor living equipment were provided by the Jacobsen Lawn & Garden Information Bureau, Jacobsen Manufacturing Co.

The discussion of the Meyersohn-Jackson nestmaking studies is based on "Gardening in Suburbia," by Rolf Meyersohn and Robin Jackson; *The Suburban Community,* edited by William Dobriner, New York, G. P. Putnam's Sons, 1958.

CHAPTER XII: The quotation about young women who try to be everything at once is taken from "What Has Succeeded Success?" by Russell Lynes. Reprinted from *Mademoiselle;* © Street and Smith Publications Inc., September, 1954.